ADVANCE *your* MOTORING

AA

ADVANCE *YOUR* MOTORING

HOW TO COPE AND CONTROL
SKID CONDITIONS ● WINTER DRIVING
MOTORWAY SAFETY ● REACTION RATES

Consultant Editor   Marcus Jacobson
MSc FIMechE MSAE MIProdE FIMI
The Automobile Association

The contents of this book
are extracted from
AA Book of Driving, edited
by Michael Buttler,
designed by Playne Design
This edition, *Advance Your Motoring*,
was previously published as Driving
Emergencies.

Produced by
the Publications Division of
the Automobile Association

Phototypeset and originated
by Sir Joseph Causton
& Sons
(Eastleigh) Ltd.

Printed and bound by
Graphicromo, S.A., Cordoba

Published by the Automobile Association, Fanum House, Basingstoke,
Hampshire RG21 2EA

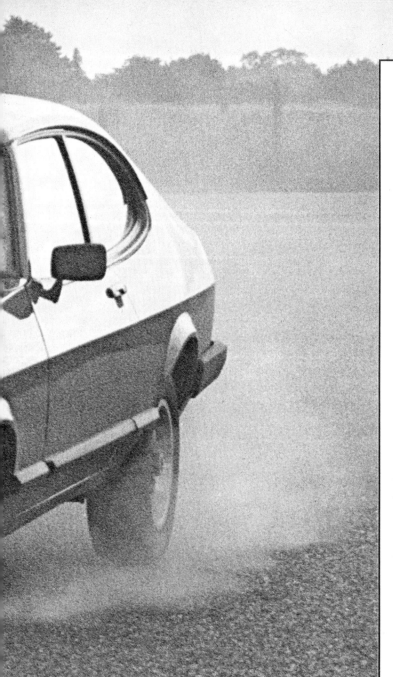

Contents

Introduction

A driving emergency can happen at any time. A situation can arise on the road where quick thinking and rapid reactions are called for at a moment's notice. Every driver hopes that this will not happen to him or her but the statistics show that most people will, sooner or later, be confronted with an emergency situation on the road.

This book sets out to show how what appears to be an emergency can be turned into a problem solved. The secrets of success are two-fold: know what you should be doing, and never give up trying to keep control. It is even better to avoid the situation in the first place by good anticipation of what other road users are doing.

The first part of the book shows the different sorts of situations that can lead to an emergency. It may be another driver's mistake or it may be a fault with your own car. In either case it is possible to plan what you would do if the unthinkable were to happen. Then, if it does, you are much better prepared. Many accidents involve skidding, and it is impossible to over-emphasise the value of being able to control the car in a skid. There are several skid training schools in different parts of the country where valuable experience in skid control can be gained.

Subsequent sections of the book show how emergencies can be avoided. Good observation, anticipation and consideration for others reduces the numbers of crises that can arise on the roads. It usually takes two to make an emergency, and if one of the two is prepared for the situation beforehand there is a much better chance of avoiding a serious accident. Every road situation is analysed, from country roads to motorways in all conditions from brilliant, dazzling sun to rain, fog, ice or snow. In each case, safe driving techniques are recommended. The driver's behaviour and reactions are crucial factors in determining how an emergency will develop. If he or she is alert and fit the chances of coping successfully with an emergency situation are greatly increased. The last section of the book tells drivers how to gauge their own level of alertness and what factors will affect them.

The high numbers of road accidents in every country in the world are horrifying. Behind every statistic is a frightening story where a driver was confronted with an emergency situation and only a short time to cope with it. Many accidents could have been avoided and we hope this book will help drivers to react quickly and correctly should the unthinkable ever happen to them.

Emergencies

Emergency situations

An unexpected situation demanding immediate action can happen to any driver at any time. A great deal can be done to prevent a situation catching a driver unawares, and it is also possible to learn how to handle such a situation safely.

Avoiding emergencies

There are some basic rules which should govern everyone's driving. If these are followed properly, few situations should develop unexpectedly.

Keep alert Driving is a task which demands full concentration. If you are being distracted, perhaps by children or pets in the car, you should stop and try to minimise the distraction. You should not drive if you feel tired, ill or unable to concentrate properly. Always expect the unexpected.

Drive within your capabilities Recognise that many factors such as your age will affect your reactions and also your eyesight, so adjust your driving accordingly. Gear your driving to the changing weather conditions.

Anticipate developments Good and thorough observation of everything that is going on all around will enable you to anticipate a situation before it develops. Feet, noticed under a parked vehicle, should warn you of the hitherto unseen presence of a pedestrian. One of the children fighting on the pavement may run in the road in front of you. A ball rolling into the road will probably be followed by a child. Any suspicion that another road user is acting dangerously or is in trouble should prompt you to slow down and give him plenty of room. Keep asking yourself what you would do if someone around you did something unexpected.

Know your car A well-maintained car should behave predictably in response to your handling, and you should be thoroughly familiar with what it will do under different conditions. The car will, of course, behave differently when it is fully laden with passengers and luggage, compared with its performance when you are driving on your own. You should also know how it will behave in response to sudden action on your part. Lack of knowledge or experience of your car's capabilities can severely hamper your reactions in an emergency.

Avoid head-on collisions A head-on collision, particularly with another moving vehicle, and even at slow speeds, will usually cause a great deal of injury and damage. If a collision is inevitable it is always preferable to try and make it a sideways scrape, or to drive obliquely on to a soft verge or through a hedge. Do not risk turning your car over, however. In every emergency situation you have a choice. Always try to minimise the danger to car passengers and other road users, before protecting the car.

Overtaking car committed to dangerous manoeuvre

Blue car brakes firmly in a straight line

When speed is low, verge is closely inspected

Blue car then steers into verge to avoid collision

Coping with an emergency

An emergency can happen at any time, so always be prepared. Careful observation and considerate driving should prevent you being taken by surprise. In spite of these precautions, you may nevertheless be presented with a situation demanding emergency action. Every situation is different, of course, but there are several points to remember in every case.

Blue car travelling at speed

There is no time to brake and stop before reaching red car

Blue car brakes in a straight line for as long as possible

Steering control must be retained to avoid red car

Do not brake too hard The instinctive reaction to an emergency is to brake hard. In some cases, however, it may be better to accelerate out of trouble. If braking is called for, apply the brakes firmly and in a straight line. Do not swerve while braking, and do not allow the wheels to lock up. If they do so, release the brakes at once, then re-apply them more sensitively. This allows you to be able to steer out of trouble to some extent.

Brake progressively rather than harshly and give the vehicle behind as much time as possible to react to your brake lights so that he will not run into the back of you. When the road surface is not dry or even, braking should always be carried out more carefully to ensure adhesion of all the tyres. If this adhesion is lost the car will get out of control, and you will no longer be able to minimise the effects of the emergency.

Always brake in a straight line, and not when you are swerving. If the wheels lock release the brakes momentarily, then apply them again. This avoids loss of control

Warn other road users Generally, other road users will be unaware that an emergency is developing, so sound your horn to warn them

Never give up Keep control of your car all the time. This will usually turn an emergency into a problem you have managed to solve.

11

Mechanical failures

Not all emergencies are produced by the behaviour of other road users. Some of them are caused by a failure of one or more of the mechanical components on a car, although this is less likely to happen if the car is properly maintained.

Should a failure occur unexpectedly, the most important consideration is to retain control of the car. Let other road users know that something is wrong by sounding the horn and switching on the lights, then check the mirrors, indicate and move to the side of the road.

Brake failure

Most modern cars have dual braking circuits so complete brake failure is unlikely. If one circuit fails, perhaps due to a break in the hydraulic pressure line, the other will usually be sufficient, although less effective.

As the speed drops gently ease the car to the side of the road and stop. Should there be insufficient time to stop using handbrake and gears, it may be necessary to scrape the side of your vehicle against walls or banks.

The brakes may become ineffective if they get wet after you have driven through a ford or a flood. Dry them by applying the brakes gently for a short distance whilst the car is moving at moderate speed. A leaking oil seal can also drastically reduce braking efficiency.

If the brakes get too hot they can also lose their effectiveness. This could happen, for example, when descending a long hill in top gear. The brake fluid may partially vaporise and the pedal would sink to the floor with little effect on the brakes. Pumping the pedal rapidly up and down frequently restores braking power.

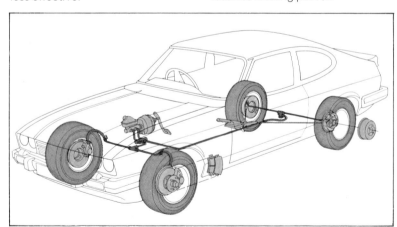

In the event of complete brake failure slow down using the handbrake and changing down quickly through the gears. Attempts to change gear too quickly or overharsh use of the handbrake can make the car unstable, however.

Should the brake pads get so hot that they 'fade', there will be no feeling of sponginess when the brake pedal is applied. A short stop usually allows them to recover, but they should be checked at the soonest opportunity.

Suspension failures

Although suspension failures are relatively rare, calm, deliberate control will prevent an accident if failure should occur. Coil springs are least prone to failure, Hydrolastic and Hydrogas units usually give some indication before they fail completely, but should a leaf spring break, it may puncture a tyre or it could sever a hydraulic pressure line.

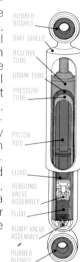

In all these eventualities let the car slow down naturally, steering and braking gently to bring the car to rest at the side of the road. Should the fuel lines or petrol tank have been damaged, avoid a possible fire by switching off the ignition and disconnecting the battery if possible. Keep well clear of the car and inform the police.

Steering failure

It is very rare indeed for steering to fail without some warning, such as an increase in steering wheel movement, or steering "wander" when attempting to keep a straight line. As soon as any of these symptoms are detected, the system should be checked by a fully qualified mechanic.

A sudden jolt to badly worn steering joints could cause them to part, resulting in steering loss. On no account try to crash stop but brake gently and progressively.

Burst tyre

If a front tyre bursts, there will be a strong pull to one side. This must be controlled by deliberate and jerk-free counter-steering to retain a straight course. A rear tyre burst may provoke a tail slide, which, again, requires restrained, smooth steering correction. In either case, do not change gear, but take your feet off the accelerator and clutch pedals, then brake gently and bring the car to a standstill. Use a hard shoulder if possible, but do not attempt to stop the car on a soft verge. A firm base will be required when jacking up the car to change the wheel.

The essentials of tyre maintenance are to keep the correct tyre pressures, to ensure that the treads are adequate and that there are no cuts or bulges in the side walls.

Loose wheel

Warnings of a wheel becoming loose are "clanking" noises and unusual handling. If these symptoms occur, slow down gently and stop. If the cause is loose wheel nuts, tighten them, then drive gently to the nearest garage where a competent mechanic can check the wheel, its nuts and bolts, wheel bearings and allied parts.

If the wheel comes off suddenly and without any warning, the car will drop at the corner affected. It will pull strongly to one side and this must be countered by firm steering and gentle, progressive braking to bring the car to a halt and prevent it slewing.

Engine failure

A frequent cause of an engine faltering is lack of fuel, usually the result of an empty tank rather than a carburettor fault. If, when the engine splutters, a quick change into a lower gear does not jerk the engine into life again, change into neutral and use the momentum of the car to move to the side of the road in order to stop. Under damp conditions a neglected ignition system can produce the same effects as lack of fuel.

Engine seizure is another matter and is often due to overheating because of a broken fan belt or lack of coolant. Increasingly poor engine response will be felt when the car slows progressively at the same throttle opening on level ground. In these circumstances pull to the side of the road as soon as it is safe to do so.

If the engine seizes up completely the driving wheels will lock up. De-clutch immediately and move the gear lever into neutral so that the car can move under its own momentum. Check the mirrors, signal and move to the side of the road, without cutting in front of another vehicle.

Bonnet flies up

This is only a problem with bonnets which open from the front of the car. There is no need to panic if this should occur. Steer on the same course, brake progressively, signal and move carefully to stop at the side of the road. Some forward vision may be obtained by winding down the driver's side window.

Windscreen shatters

Laminated windscreens present little problem as they remain transparent even after an impact by a stone causing nothing more than a star-shaped scar. Toughened glass screens usually incorporate a zone in front of the driver which gives fair visibility even when the rest of the screen cannot be seen through with clarity.

Toughened windscreen

When the windscreen shatters do not punch a hole through it immediately. Check your mirrors, signal, move gently to the side of the road and stop when it is safe to do so. Remove as much of the broken glass as possible by pushing it out onto a sheet or newspaper on the bonnet. Do not push the glass into the car interior or allow it to block any heater vents.

Impact on laminated windscreen

A temporary windscreen will allow you to proceed safely, but if you do not have one you can still drive, although with great care and at a low speed. In that eventuality make sure that all the glass fragments have been removed from the windscreen surround.

Accelerator sticks down

A first reaction to this problem is to try to get a toe under the pedal and lift it. In many cases, however, the cause is a broken throttle return spring and the pedal stays down.

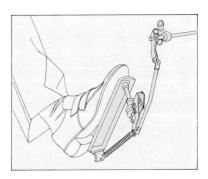

The appropriate action is to check mirrors, move the gear lever into neutral, then signal left. Switch off the ignition, but do not withdraw the ignition key as this can lock the steering, then coast to the side of the road, and stop.

Maintenance saves emergencies

A check of the tyres, brakes and steering at the start of every journey, plus regular maintenance and the immediate replacement of any suspect components would prevent most of the emergencies described here from taking place.

Emergency problem

How would you react if you were faced with an emergency situation. Having read about the subject you would know enough to deal with the situation in theory. Would your reflexes be quick enough to assess and review every option to you and still leave you enough time to adopt the right course?

Imagine you are confronted with the situation described on this page. It is based on an incident which actually happened, although the details have been changed. In the real incident a collision was avoided. What would you have done in this situation?

You are driving a family car towards a cross-channel port en route for a summer holiday abroad. The sun is shining, the road is dry and smooth. About 15 miles before the port you enter a built-up area. The speed restriction is 40mph, the road has two wide lanes bordered by normal width pavement and kerbing, with fences beyond.

Driving at a safe 35mph you approach a left hand bend. Buildings on your left restrict forward vision to around 50 yards. You have taken up a position to the left of the centre line in order to obtain the best view through the bend. On entering the bend you find an oncoming car driving directly towards you on your side of the road.

You sound your horn to alert the other driver. Generally, you will have been driving with sufficient care and anticipation to avoid an accident, but in this case the other driver makes no attempt to steer his car back to his own side of the road. In the first split-second you notice that it carries a French registration plate.

Approaching the bend at 35 mph visibility is restricted to 50 yards. At first all seems clear

Suddenly an oncoming car is seen approaching on the wrong side of the road

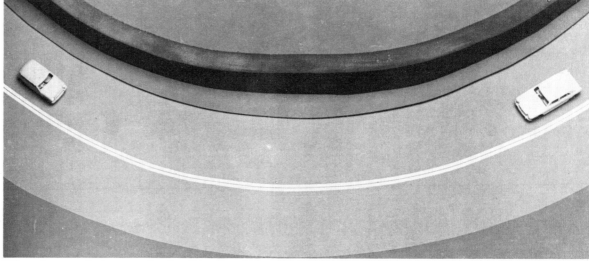

When the cars first see each other 1½ seconds are left for avoiding action

What would you do?

a Freeze up completely

b Brake hard
c Swerve to the right
d Swerve to the left

e Brake firmly and swerve out of the way at the last moment when you see where the other driver moves.

a It will be too late to avoid a head-on collision if you do not react instantly. Suppose both cars are travelling at 35mph, the closing speed is 70mph or about 34 yards a second. When the two cars are 50 yards apart, there are about 1½ seconds in which to take positive avoiding action.

b Panic braking will lock up the front wheels and the car will slide straight on with no steering control at all, or the rear end may break away and the car will slew. It would be impossible to swerve out of the way at any point.

c A sudden swerve to the right can easily result in loss of control. If the back wheels start to slide there will be a collision.

d A sudden swerve to the left could also result in a loss of control. In this case it would also have resulted in a head-on collision. The oncoming car was, indeed, French. He had just come off a cross-channel ferry and had not yet oriented himself to driving on the left hand side of the road.

The fact that the driver made no attempt to return to the correct side of the road even after your horn warning confirms that this is so and also that he believes he is perfectly in the right. In fact, his reaction to the situation is to behave as he would have done at home, and he swerves to his right, (your left) and into the kerb. If you had swerved left, you would certainly have hit him.

e The correct response is to get your speed right down while keeping firm control of the car.

Knowing you were near a port would, in any case, have fore-warned you to expect some cars to be on the wrong side of the road. You will have been driving with the appropriate degree of caution when this incident arose and have been prepared to react quickly if necessary. Firstly, avoid any kind of panic reaction.

Brake firmly in a straight line, but not so hard that you lock the wheels and lose control. At this point the other driver begins his turn towards your left. With your speed now much reduced, and steering under control, you turn your car to the right, towards the centre of the road, thus avoiding contact. A careful study of the situation as it developed, while remaining firmly in control of the car, enabled you to react quickly but without panic.

Initially, brake firmly in a straight line

Steer right when you see what the other car does

Preparation for emergencies

Everyone can prepare themselves to cope with emergencies. Each time you go out in a car, whether as the driver or not, you should observe and study the road in order to anticipate what will develop. Accurate anticipation often prevents emergencies. Keep asking yourself what you would do if the situation ahead of you changed suddenly and dramatically.

You should take every opportunity to practise and improve your car control. This should not be done on a public road but on a specialised training area, skid-pan, or on a disused airfield.

Several specialist courses are available in advanced and high speed driving and these are extremely useful as a start towards preparing yourself to deal with emergencies. A most valuable feature of these courses is that they reveal any weaknesses or bad habits in your driving, enabling you to overcome them. After that, continue to practise the relevant techniques.

Anticipation and control

Most emergency situations can be prevented by good observation and intelligent anticipation. Careful reading of the road scene and gentle car handling should ensure that you enter each situation at the right speed and in perfect control.

Reading the road well ahead enables you to spot hold-ups such as lorries turning in good time, so you can avoid braking harshly

When following a large vehicle, particularly on a narrow road, keep a safe distance behind and when possible look along its nearside

Observing the road beyond the lorry would have given you advance warning of the parked car and helped avoid sudden manoeuvres

Sharp observation is needed when driving in busy streets to spot the pedestrians stepping into the road, as well as other hazards

Seeing the broken-down lorry in plenty of time helps you make an early lane change, minimising disruption to traffic flow

The parked van actually conceals some road works, as the observant driver will have noted from the warning sign ahead

Braking

The general rules about braking, whether in an emergency situation or not are :
1. Brake in plenty of time.
2. Brake firmly only when travelling in a straight line.
3. Vary the brake pressure according to the condition of the road surface

When preparing to handle a possible future emergency situation, an important aspect of car control to practise is braking from speed. You should know just how hard you can brake in your car without locking the wheels and losing steering control.

Practise, off the public roads, driving at a series of different speeds, then slowing the car down in a straight line by adjusting the braking pressures. When you have mastered control at one speed try a slightly higher one.

Once you can control the braking of your car from speed, start gently swerving to one side while braking and keeping steering control at all times. This will increase your confidence in your own driving ability and will help you to react positively to emergencies.

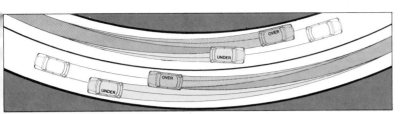

Under-steer

A small degree of understeering characteristics are designed into most modern cars. This gives them stability in a straight line at speed, under crosswind conditions and also when cornering.

The front of the car tends to run wider than the curve of the bend and this must be countered by greater movement of the steering in the direction of the bend.

Over-steer

The behaviour of an over-steering car on a bend is the opposite of one with understeer. The car tends to turn in towards the bend, because the centrifugal force moves the rear of the car outwards. This requires a steering correction in order to maintain control. An oversteering car will not have the inherent stability of an understeering one in gusty crosswinds, and will need constant steering correction. Correction will also be required on roads with pronounced changes in road cambers.

As the speed at which a bend is taken is increased, so the steering characteristics of a car will change. One which normally has a degree of understeer will, at high speed on a corner, develop neutral steer and then change to over-steer. This transition should, ideally, be progressive and predictable. If it takes place too rapidly it can be unexpected and dangerous.

Car care

However proficient the driver in coping with an emergency, it is essential that the car behaves and responds reliably and as expected. This is only achieved if it is maintained in good condition.

Great stress will be thrown on the brakes, tyres, steering and hydraulic dampers in dealing with an emergency, and these should always be kept in first class condition. The driving exercises above will indicate whether any of them is deficient.

Brakes If these are not working at full efficiency, it will take you longer to stop. Have the brakes and brake fluid levels checked regularly and do not wait to replace friction linings until they are worn down.

Tyres The steering response can be critically affected by the wrong, or incorrectly inflated, tyres. Tyre pressures should be checked regularly, and tyres inspected for signs of over- or under-inflation.

Hydraulic dampers Weak dampers can cause the car to pitch badly with an increased tendency to roll. This can seriously affect braking and steering, particularly in an emergency situation.

Windscreen A clean windscreen free from smears will aid observation and visibility, particularly if an emergency should arise. Good windscreen wipers and an effective screen wash are also important.

Headlights Properly adjusted headlights will maximise your own vision when driving at night, and also minimise dazzle to others.

Seat belts Make sure your seat belts work properly, and, if you have children, install approved safety restraints to the back seat. Never allow a child to travel in the front seat.

Parcel shelf Keep the rear parcel shelf free from loose objects which could fly forward during a collision, into the necks of the driver or passengers. Even light objects can be dangerous if propelled with enough force.

Roll-over bar If driving an open car have a roll-over bar fitted. If a car without one turns over, the occupants have no protection.

Skidding

No good driver should ever find his car skidding unintentionally. A skid is usually the result of poor observation, too high a speed, harsh use of the controls or a badly-maintained car. Knowing how to control a skid is essential, however, since even a good driver may skid sometime.

Four wheel skid

When harsh braking locks all four wheels and the car skids, the only way to regain control is to release the brakes and then re-apply them more gently. This allows the tyres to roll again and re-establish their grip on the road. If the steering is not straight ahead, it is important to straighten up before trying to get back on course.

Skid control is not taught to learner drivers, and for many people the first skid will be a completely unexpected experience. The most important consideration is not to panic. Look in the direction you want to go, not where you appear to be going. The next thing to remember is not to over-correct a skid. It is better to let the car sort itself out than to induce a secondary skid by over-correction. Most modern cars respond very quickly to ·even a slight steering correction. Radial ply tyres react in a fraction of the time that cross-plies used to do, at a fraction of the steering input formerly required.

Tyre grip

A skid is caused when a tyre loses its grip on the road surface and starts sliding instead of rolling. As soon as this happens, control of the car is lost. The area of contact between tyre and road is very small, no bigger than a size 9 shoe. It is critical that this small area remains effective.

The tread of the tyre is an important factor in retaining grip, particularly if the road is not dry. Water on the road surface is dispelled by the channels and slots of the tread pattern so that the tyre can grip on the road surface proper.

Suspension and steering

The design of the car's suspension and steering are inter-related and have important effects upon its handling.

Worn dampers cause unsteady cornering, a bumpy ride when on the move and unpleasant dipping movement when braking. The tyres may not be kept in sufficiently close contact with the road surface and skidding is much more likely to occur. Badly misaligned steering geometry can also increase the risks of skidding.

Road surfaces

A good appreciation of the nature of the road surface and its camber is an important aspect of skid prevention. In fine weather, dust or gravel on the surface can dramatically reduce tyre adhesion, as can mud on country roads. Light rain on roads which have been dry for some time causes a potentially dangerous situation. The rain water can mix with the oily and rubber deposits which are lying on the road surface to form a very slippery surface, and a mixture which could block up the tyre tread.

Rain on the road surface will obviously reduce tyre adhesion. Autumn and winter bring their own skid hazards to road surfaces. Fallen leaves in the autumn produce a very slippery surface.

Road observation

Accurate reading of the road ahead and to the side will prevent most skids, particularly in adverse weather. Judging the severity of an approaching bend is not always easy, but the line of the roadside hedge in the distance can provide an indication. Do not always trust the line of telegraph posts, however, as these can sometimes cut straight across a field, while the road bends in a different direction.

Smooth handling

Skids can be induced or made worse by harsh or sudden braking, harsh acceleration, jerky steering and excessive speed. If the car handling were carried out more smoothly and with greater delicacy, the risks of skidding would be halved. Too heavy a grip on the steering wheel is sometimes a cause of harsh car handling.

Wheelspin

The definition of a skid, in which the grip of the tyre on the road surface is lost, could include wheelspin, with which most drivers are familiar. It is usually caused by harsh use of the accelerator, and can only be cured by easing off. Continuing to press the accelerator will not increase the chances of getting a grip on the road.

Front wheel skid

The car tends to travel straight on in this type of skid despite the direction in which the driver is trying to steer. It is usually brought on by harsh acceleration into a corner, when the front wheels lose their grip. It may seem as though the steering has failed, but do not attempt to apply more steering lock. The first thing to do is to take your foot off the accelerator. Then straighten up the front wheels, so that they can start rotating again. Once grip has been restored steer gently in the direction you wish to take.

This steering correction must be applied very briefly and very gently. Over-correction could result in a rear wheel skid which will be very difficult to control. On no account apply the brakes.

Front wheel drive cars

When a front wheel drive car gets into a front wheel skid, do not take your foot off the accelerator suddenly, as this would have the effect of braking. Reduce the acceleration, but keep a light pressure. Continue to steer into the corner until the car regains its course, then gently start to increase the acceleration.

Rear wheel skid

When driving too fast round a corner or bend, the rear of the car may break away and cause a rear wheel skid. The commonly-stated advice is 'steer into the skid', but this is not always easy to interpret.

Modern radial ply tyres and recent types of suspension system are extremely quick to respond to a skid. They can react a great deal more quickly than most drivers will be able to. Steel-braced tyres generate a self-straightening effect very much more quickly than older generation tyres, particularly cross plies. For the same steering correction, steel-braced tyres will develop up to three times the sideways guidance force that cross ply tyres used to do. This sideways guidance force restores straight line running.

Because of these developments in tyre technology, it is now frequently the best course of action to take your foot off the accelerator (do not touch the brake or clutch pedals). Apply only very slight steering correction for a short time, very quickly but not jerkily. Do not attempt to steer into the skid for any length of time since this could provoke a dangerous aggravation of the skid. As soon as possible return to a neutral steering position.

A major danger with this type of skid is over-reaction, resulting in excessive correction of the initial skid. A secondary skid is set up, often worse than the first one, and this again could provoke excessive steering response. The result can easily be a 'sawing' motion of the steering wheel, rapidly leading to loss of control.

It is not necessary to grip the steering wheel more tightly than usual during skid control. A light but firm handhold is preferable, and allows the car's course, once it starts to skid to be corrected quickly and accurately without nearly so much risk of over-correction.

One cause of a front wheel skid   *Demonstration of how a rear wheel skid would be induced and controlled on a skid-pan*

Skid-pans

Practice at recognising a skid and learning to control it can only be gained on a skid-pan. This is a specially prepared area, set away from public roads, where members of the public may learn about skids. Unfortunately there are not many skid-pans in existence, partly because they are expensive to run and seldom attract sufficient support. Their value, however, cannot be over-estimated.

Skid-pan construction

The surface of a skid-pan is usually designed to give minimum tyre grip, especially when the surface is wet, as it normally will be. In some cases, in addition to watering, the surface will have been specially treated to deliberately induce slipperiness.

It is often the case that you do not use your own car, but one which is supplied. This may be fitted with 'slick' tyres which have no tread at all, so skids will happen at low speed. Occasionally, after completing a course of instruction, you may be encouraged to take your own car on to the skid-pan to discover how it handles.

The skid-pan is coated with special compounds to facilitate skidding.

Instruction

Different arrangements are made at every skid-pan. In some cases the sessions last several hours and include lectures and demonstrations. In others, the sessions are one hour or less. The use of the skid-pan may be linked to a course on better driving run by the Local Authority. The qualified instructors may come from the Police, the Institute of Advanced Motorists or be Approved Driving Instructors. Details of current opening times, charges, how the courses are organised, the use of your own car, etc., are best obtained from your local Road Safety Officer.

Recognising a skid

One of the advantages of a skid-pan is that it teaches you what the onset of a skid feels like. This is particularly valuable if you have not experienced it before. Failing to recognise that a skid is developing, and thus reacting to it too slowly or too abruptly are common causes of loss of control in a skid. It is important to recognise it quickly and to respond smoothly and in good time.

In some ways a skid-pan gives an artificial idea of what a skid is like. The treated surface means that a skid is induced at a relatively low speed. In addition, however, you will be expecting a skid to occur on a skid-pan. Some skid-pans have one area treated differently from the rest to make things less predictable. This will teach you how to cope with differing degrees of adhesion.

Familiarity with the sensation of skidding, achieved through practice on a skid-pan, is the first step to avoiding the panic over-reaction which so often occurs. The results of over-correction of a skid will become apparent at an early stage and you can then learn to appreciate how effective the strategy is of making only the minimum necessary steering corrections, taking the feet off all the pedals and letting the tyres correct the skid.

Another important benefit of skid-pan experience is that you learn to recognise the point at which control has been regained. Just as you will feel when tyre to road grip becomes marginal, that is when a skid is about to happen, so you will be able to tell that you have regained control. Skid-pan practice will accustom you to the feeling of skids of different types.

Practising cornering on a skid-pan. By avoiding a front wheel skid control is retained through the bend

Skid practice

A skid-pan provides an opportunity to keep practising a particular type of skid until it is familiar and understood. In most real life situations, however, events will happen much more quickly for loss of tyre grip will occur at higher speeds.

A **front wheel skid** can be provoked by turning the steering wheel and braking hard. The front wheels will lock and steering control will be lost. By releasing the brakes, some steering control will be restored and you can practise trying to keep to a proper steering line.

A **rear wheel skid** can be provoked simply by going a little too fast round the skid-pan circuit. It can also be induced at a moderate speed by turning the steering wheel, pulling the handbrake on briefly and then releasing it. This will lock the rear wheels while retaining front wheel grip, and the rear of the car will slew. Take your foot off the accelerator, do not touch the brake or clutch pedals, apply any necessary steering correction, then return the steering to a neutral position until control of the car is regained.

A more advanced driver can use the skid-pan to make the basic manoeuvre from which to engineer more problems, allowing the driver to improve his skill further. It is possible, for example, to learn the knack of sliding the car from lock to lock under complete control, while maintaining speed by keeping the foot on the throttle.

A rear wheel skid is provoked on the curve. Skid-pan practice will enable it to be controlled

Emergency Quiz

It may be easy to feel that the essentials of skid control are understood after reading about them in a book. Experience on the road is very different, and can be assisted by practice gained on a skid-pan. One way to check whether you would do the right thing if you were involved in a skid is to try the quiz on this page. Although the answers are given here, try to work out your own answer before reading them.

1 What are the factors that could cause a skid?

2 Which pedal must you not press when you have got into a skid?

3 Which pedal would you press in a car with a manual gear box if you get into a skid?

4 In the event of a rear wheel skid on a left hand bend with the car sliding to your right, in which direction would you turn the steering wheel?

5 What effect do weak shock absorbers have on road adhesion?

6 Under what road conditions are you most likely to skid?

7 What should you do if, when braking for a bend, your front wheels lock up?

8 In a similar situation what should you do if the front wheels start to skid outwards towards the crown of the road?

9 What is a secondary skid and how is it caused?

10 Is a front-wheel-drive car more prone to front wheel skidding than either a front engine rear-wheel-drive car or a rear engine car?

11 What should you do if a front-wheel-drive car gets into a front wheel skid?

12 How would you deliberately induce a skid on a skid-pan?

13 What is the most important aspect of skid-pan practice?

14 What is done to some skid-pans to give varying degrees of adhesion?

15 Which tyres, radials or cross-plies, have better cornering power?

16 Why do bald or badly-worn tyres lose adhesion on wet roads?

17 Apart from bald tyres, what other tyre conditions contribute to skids?

18 What tyres should you fit to your car to minimise the chance of any form of skid?

19 What is the essence of skid prevention for a driver?

20 In the event of getting into a skid what is the first requirement of the driver?

Answers

1 Poor driving involving perhaps driving too fast, insufficiently good observation of the road ahead or harsh use of controls.

2 The brake pedal. Applying the brakes in a skid will tend to lock up the wheels, making it even more difficult to regain control. Control is only regained when the tyres are in rolling contact with the road surface. The best strategy when in a skid is not to press any of the pedals at all.

3 It has sometimes been suggested that depressing the clutch may help, but as stated in the answer to question 2, it is better not to press any of the pedals. You may get into another skid when you let in the clutch.

4 Any movement of the steering wheel must be carried out as soon as the slide is detected, and then with great care. In this case, steer slightly to the right, enough to 'catch' the slide, then return the steering to a neutral position. Do not steer too far to the right, or keep the steering in that position for more than a very short time or the car will start to slide to the left.

5 Weak shock absorbers allow the wheels to bounce excessively on the road surface. This means that road contact is only poorly maintained, resulting in reduced tyre-to-road adhesion. They will also cause imbalance in the car's handling.

6 Under almost any road condition if you are inattentive. In general terms, anything on the road surface which is loose such as gravel, anything which will provide a film between the tyre and the road, such as rain or ice, increases the risk of skidding. Particularly hazardous is light rain after a long dry spell. This spreads a film of water over a surface covered with an oily, rubber deposit and the road becomes extremely slippery.

7 Release the brakes for a fraction of a second to regain steering control, then re-apply them more sensitively.

8 Release the accelerator and straighten up the steering so that, for a very short time you are steering in the direction of the skid. Once steering control has been regained continue your course round the corner. Do not brake under any circumstances.

9 A secondary skid is caused by over-correcting the first skid, either by applying too harsh a steering correction or continuing it for too long. The result is to make the car go from one skid to another on the other side, the second usually more difficult to control than the first.

10 The idea that all front-wheel-drive cars have superior road-holding to other cars is not borne out in practice.

11 You should ease off the accelerator smoothly, but not completely. A small amount of power should still be applied to the front wheels. Otherwise, removal of the power can have a braking effect which could result in the rear of the car breaking away.

12 There are several ways of doing this. Driving too fast into a curve will provoke a skid, so will steering into a curve and braking hard or steering left or right and pulling very hard on the handbrake.

13 To get used to the feeling of the car's loss of adhesion. Once you can recognise the onset of a skid you will be able to react quickly and smoothly enough to control it before it goes too far. Practice in dealing with the different types of skid is also most important.

14 Certain sections of the skid-pan may be treated with a liquid having a low co-efficient of friction or may have a permanent special surface treatment which simulates a greasy patch offering less adhesion than other parts.

15 Radial ply tyres have better cornering performance as a built-in feature.

16 The tread of a tyre dispels the water lying on the road so that the tyre can grip on the surface below. When the tread is very thin or absent, the tyre cannot make such good contact with the road surface even at low speeds. At high speeds the tyre may 'float' off the surface and aquaplane.

17 Underinflated tyres distort excessively when cornering and this reduces their grip on the road surface. Unevenly worn tyres offer reduced tyre to road grip. Unequal pressure distribution side to side can also promote the onset of a skid.

18 In most cases you should fit the tyres recommended by your car's manufacturer, but you should seek the advice of a tyre specialist before changing to anything very different.

19 To read the road well ahead, to be at the right speed and in the right gear for every situation, especially when cornering. You should always bear in mind the road surface conditions at the time, whether the road is dry, or covered in rain, mud or ice.

20 The first requirement is not to panic. If you can think quickly and clearly and recognise the type of skid involved you are well on the way to taking the correct action. Remembering that modern car and tyre design is such that a great deal of the correction will be carried out automatically by the car itself without active participation of the driver, you should try to make any steering correction precisely and smoothly. This is better than reacting suddenly and losing all control.

Skilled driving

Driving with consideration

Better driving consists of more than merely equipping yourself to handle situations as they arise. The better driver is also a courteous driver who exercises consideration for the particular requirements of different road users. This consideration will usually also result in smoother traffic flow.

Old people should be given extra consideration. Their eyesight may be poor, their movements slow, they may be deaf, and they could be absorbed in their own affairs. Allowing them to cross the road in front of you is a simple courtesy, provided it is safe for them to cross and that other traffic realises what is happening.

Children are one of the most vulnerable groups of road users. This sign warns, not of a school, but of some other area such as a playground where children will be found. Young children cannot accurately estimate the speeds of approaching traffic and their size often limits what they can see along the road. When they are playing their minds concentrate exclusively on the game and they are oblivious to passing traffic. These are only three reasons why the presence of children near the road requires great caution.

Pedestrians on country lanes must often walk in the road. They should walk so that they face oncoming traffic, but this is sometimes not the case. Drive at such a speed that you do not endanger them should you meet opposing traffic. Especial care is required at night when pedestrians may be wearing dark clothing and are obscured.

Cyclists should be given a wide berth, and if you cannot give them plenty of space when overtaking you should stay behind them until it is safe to do so. When starting off, or on hills, they may wobble from side to side, but do not startle them with a sudden horn blast or there is the risk that they might fall off in your path.

Keep a close watch out for motorcyclists. Although they are not very wide they move at least as fast as other traffic and are sometimes barely visible. Many of them use their headlights to make themselves more conspicuous, but this is by no means universal. Give them plenty of room as the slightest touch can overturn them.

Taxis behave unexpectedly from time to time, stopping or turning suddenly in order to pick up or set down fares.

Horse riding is an increasingly popular pursuit and horses on the road should be approached with great restraint. Any horn blast could frighten them and make them rear, so pass them quietly without revving the engine.

Delivery vans of all kinds can be expected to obstruct traffic from time to time, but milk floats travel extremely slowly. They may turn across the road unexpectedly, and, in residential areas, pedestrians may walk towards them without considering the traffic.

All buses should be treated with care and consideration. Any sign of bus passengers preparing to alight will signal the approach of a bus stop to an observant driver, probably before the bus stop itself is visible. Beware of pedestrians crossing the road to or from the bus when it has stopped and allow the driver to move off and join the traffic stream when he is ready to do so.

Emergency vehicles should always be given priority. Any indication of their presence, such as a siren or flashing lights, should prompt you to keep well to the left, preparing to stop if necessary in order to let them through.

Observation

One of the most important ways to develop better and safer driving is to cultivate the skill of sharp observation. This entails more than just looking at the road in front of you. It involves looking also to the side and rear, and studying the road ahead in a particular way.

The experienced driver will constantly shift his gaze, from side to side and along the road ahead, between a point close to the car right along to the horizon. He will also regularly look in his rear view mirrors. The less experienced driver will tend to concentrate his attention on a point not very far in front of the car. Because of this, every new development will arise very suddenly and will often catch him unprepared to respond.

Maximum information about any road scene is obtained in several ways. Apart from assessing the behaviour of all the vehicles and other road users in sight, additional aspects can sometimes be seen by looking along the nearside or offside of the vehicles in front or, according to the road layout, under them or over them. It is frequently possible to see through the rear and front windows of private cars and passengers can sometimes be seen preparing to alight from a bus. All these methods help the driver find out as much as possible about the road situation ahead.

The road markings provide the observant driver with a great deal of information about the road ahead and any hazards coming up.

The centre line markings change from a short, dashed, white line to a series of longer, white dashes. This warns of the approach to a hazard which is the sharp right-hand bend ahead where the side road joins.

The path of the road ahead, particularly in country areas, can often be inferred from the line of hedges or telegraph poles. At times other traffic can be seen a considerable distance away.

When passing a line of parked cars, always look into each one to see if there is a driver at the wheel or a passenger likely to open a door. Look for signs of exhaust smoke or wheels turning which indicate that a car may be pulling out. In this street, near a school, be prepared for small children, concealed by the cars, to suddenly run into the road right in front of you.

Looking along this line of cars, we see that the driver can be seen in the car just ahead, and that he is beginning to open the driver's door. In view of the oncoming traffic you should slow down before reaching him.

The scene ahead demands great caution. As well as the horses a dog can be seen running loose in the road. Be prepared to find more horses round the left-hand bend, but do not hoot or startle them.

The sight of a play area, especially if it is unfenced, should alert you to the possible presence of children near the road when you get round the corner ahead.

Housing estates require cautious driving and careful observation. A group of children can be seen by looking through the windows of the parked car. Children often play in the road on housing estates so watch carefully for any indication of their presence.

Watch out for the dog off the lead on this busy road. If he were to run into your path, several vehicles could be caught unawares, so ease off the power earlier than you otherwise would when approaching this junction. You should also be checking that the parked van is not likely to move out obstructing your path.

Additional information about the road ahead can be obtained from the reflections in shop windows. This is particularly valuable for obtaining early warning about other traffic at times when your own view is obscured by other vehicles or by a bend in the road.

Anticipation

The better driver uses the art of good observation by developing a keen sense of anticipation. Not only should you look carefully all round you for any information you can glean about a developing situation, but you should also look for clues which will help you anticipate what will happen next. This awareness will enable you to adjust your driving so that you do not have to take sudden action, possibly endangering other road users as well as yourself.

The road itself will give you several clues as to its likely path. A right-hand bend is coming up ahead, and those skid marks on the approach tell you it must be sharper than it appears. You can thus slow down in good time.

In winter beware of concealed patches of ice. You can anticipate that they are likely to be present on those portions of the road overhung by branches.

Read the road ahead for any indications of likely hazards. Just before the left-hand bend ahead, a signpost can be seen warning of a turning on the right. You can anticipate that traffic may turn out of it, and this, indeed, proves to be the case.

Side turnings, especially farm entrances, are not always signposted on country roads, but their existence can sometimes be anticipated. The road ahead looks clear and free from any side turnings, but the fence visible in the field on the left is, in fact, a warning to the observant driver that a farm entrance is coming up.

Due notice should always be taken of road signs, and the flashing amber lights on this school sign warn that children are on their way to and from school. Be prepared to have to stop for them—this is obligatory when a school crossing patrol holds up the sign with the warning 'Stop—Children'.

This sign announces the presence of roadworks, but none are visible. Anticipate that they could be masked by the parked van and expect to find workmen or lorries obstructing the road just behind it. Adjust your speed as you approach the van in case this happens and give as much clearance as possible.

Always look well ahead of you for advance warning of developing situations. A van can be seen parked on the left side of the road. On the opposite side can be seen a pedestrian. Anticipating that he will walk across the road to the van will prepare you for this situation when it happens.

When driving through a housing estate be prepared for children and animals who will not be expecting much traffic. Small children may suddenly come round a corner on bicycles or chasing a ball. The appearance of one child is often an indication that others are not far behind, so slow down immediately. Children are seldom good at assessing the speed of approaching traffic.

Whenever you see an ice cream van parked anticipate that it will be a magnet for children. In this incident a young girl ran to it, without looking, right across the road in front of the car in order to get her ice cream.

This scene looks quiet and trouble-free. The main road appears to continue down a dip when it is concealed from view and then uphill on the other side. A vehicle can be seen descending the hill before the dip. The edge of a red triangular warning sign can be seen, however, and this should warn us of something unexpected. As we get closer to the dip in the road, we are warned that it contains a cross roads, but it is not until we are much closer that we see the signpost indicating that the major road turns right here. Looking well ahead while driving can warn of impending situations such as this. Early anticipation that it is not completely straightforward should have led you to proceed with caution into the dip, giving you plenty of time to prepare for the junction.

Driving commentary

The art of better driving is extremely well illustrated by a driving commentary. This consists of a running commentary made while driving, and embraces your observations, present driving behaviour and plans for future tactics. Even when driving on your own, a spoken commentary will confirm that you are putting the principles of better driving into action. A good commentary takes a great deal of practice to perfect, and an example is given here based on a typical cross-country journey involving several different types of road environment.

We are driving along a minor country road. The weather is dry and sunny, casting shadows across the road. There are no central line markings on the stretch in front of us and the nearside edge is badly broken up. We are approaching a sharp right hand bend with hedges concealing any opposing traffic. Looking in our mirror we see there is no traffic behind us and we slow to 25 mph, changing into third gear to negotiate the bend.

The road has widened now with centre line markings and long, straight stretches. Approaching a cross roads the centre line markings become warning lines and we can see a car waiting to emerge from the right. We ease off the power in case he moves out.

We note the staggered cross roads sign, and as we approach the junction we see a parked car blocking a portion of the road just before a left bend. We take up a position just to the left of the centre line in order to see as far as possible into the bend.

At first glance it appears as though the road goes straight on but there is in fact a sharp right hand bend. We have just passed a school sign and now deduce from the existence of the bus shelter that we are on a bus route.

Approaching the brow of a hill with warning line markings and an obscured road sign ahead we check the mirrors and slow, preparing to change down. It turns out to have a steep downhill gradient of 1 in 5.

The road is narrow with straight stretches. Ahead is a long vehicle and two cars are opposing. The centre line markings change to warning line markings so there must be a hazard ahead, perhaps a turning to the farm buildings visible on the right.

Coming up behind this slow-moving tractor we do not try to overtake it. He is signalling left and a car can be seen waiting to emerge from the right. Traffic on this road may include horse riders, so we keep our speed down.

Coming to this parked car we slow right down. There are road works and a petrol station beyond it, but we give a brief horn signal to make the people standing in the road aware of our presence.

We are on the outskirts of a town with cars parked on both sides of the road. Two cars ahead are blocking the left portion of the road as they turn into and out of driveways. We cannot see if any of the other parked cars intend to move and we ease off the power.

We are approaching red traffic lights and note the presence of the right-turning lane. The car in front of us is indicating left, but no left turning can be seen at the traffic lights, so we check in the mirror for traffic behind and prepare for him to stop at the side of the road.

In this side road we give way to an oncoming bus. He flashes his lights at us, but we wait until we are absolutely certain of his meaning before moving. It becomes clear he wishes us to come on, so we check the mirrors, signal and move forward without further delay.

The road is now a dual carriageway and we are approaching the end of it where we can see a petrol station, a shopping area and a set of traffic lights. We prepare for traffic moving into or out of the petrol station.

Driving through a shopping area we take the opportunity to look along the nearside of the van in front for possible hazards. We see a pedestrian waiting at the kerb to cross on the Pelican crossing and prepare to stop.

Leaving the town we approach a cross roads just before the derestriction signs. No traffic is waiting to emerge, but the motorcyclist seems uncertain of his intentions. We slow to allow him plenty of room to manoeuvre.

Continuing towards the town, we pass a zebra crossing and see a car waiting in a side road on the left. The traffic is not heavy, but, out of courtesy, we allow him to feed into the traffic stream in front of us.

At this set of traffic lights a group of pedestrians is waiting on the central island. We check that they have seen us and that no small children are concealed behind the bollards.

The road widens to a dual carriageway; the car in front is turning left and the road ahead appears clear after that.

Country roads

The extensive network of minor roads linking rural communities and the main cross-country routes are seldom as peaceful and relaxing to drive along as they may seem. Agricultural and other country traffic which use them can pose situations requiring degrees of concentration and anticipation every bit as high as driving on more major roads.

Road surfaces

Many country roads have a relatively poor surface, although there are outstanding exceptions. The edges may be crumbling and potholed. The roads will also be susceptible to frost damage.

Farm machinery which has been working in muddy fields will lay a

Visibility

The twists and bends of narrow country roads often restrict long distance visibility. This is made worse by the high hedges which sometimes line the sides of the roads in rural areas.

Drivers should proceed along this type of road at a speed conducive to safety. Slow-moving traffic may be encountered round any corner on a country road. The use of the horn on approaching blind, narrow bends is a wise precaution.

Wherever the road layout permits, try to look over and beyond hedges or any other sight restrictions. This can give an early indication of the path the road will follow, and sometimes high vehicles, such as tractors can be seen well in advance down the road.

trail of mud when it returns to a properly surfaced road. If you see tractors working in a field, expect to find mud on the road ahead of you. This may happen even in dry, sunny weather and the trail may continue for a considerable distance. Any dirt or mud on the road surface could cause a skid in an emergency.

Road works

Because they are so important as links in the rural community, local councils usually carry out maintenance and repair work on country roads a short section at a time. This may involve re-laying the surface of the road, but it can also be hedge-trimming, laying sewerage pipes, or reinforcing the edges. It is sometimes possible to obtain early warning of road works from a glimpse of the metal cab top

of a lorry or the tip of a metal exhaust stack seen over the tops of the hedges.

Hazards on the road

Very narrow roads may not be sufficiently wide for two vehicles to pass each other. These will usually be signed as such on the approach and will have passing places set into them at periodic intervals. On a hill, always allow the traffic going up the hill to have priority, particularly if it is a heavy vehicle.

Occasionally, a road will be found which has a gate across it. This is usually placed there in order to prevent cattle wandering outside the area. The gate should always be closed after you have passed it, even if it was open at the time you approached.

When harvest time is over, farmers frequently burn off the stubble. Although this may seem a dramatic and attractive sight, be prepared for dense smoke reducing visibility down the road.

Driving at night on country roads can be easier than on other roads. The use of headlights is universal and the discipline of the drivers to dip their headlights is usually good, although speeds tend to be slow. Headlights flashed when approaching corners or humps in the road give advance warning of your presence to other traffic. Oncoming traffic can be seen from some distance, as the light from their headlights will be visible above the highest hedge.

Some country roads may be broken by a ford, often near a village. Several of these have a depth

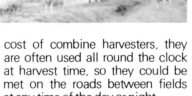

Farm animals

If you see animals grazing in a field, be alert to the possibility that it may be milking time, or that a shepherd might be moving a flock of sheep from one pasture to another. Either of these activities if met with on the road must be faced with patience and the animals allowed to pass safely. Impatience may result in the animals damaging your car.

Cattle and sheep graze wild in moorland countryside for months on end, and it is not uncommon to find animals literally lying in the road. Great care must be exercised in these circumstances.

Horses

Horses being ridden on the road should be treated with great caution. Even the best trained horse may shy at a sudden noise or the sound of a car. As you approach, slow right down and be prepared to stop if necessary. If it is not possible to pass the animal safely, stop well behind it until the approaching vehicle is past. Drive past the horse slowly, quietly and giving it as wide a berth as possible.

gauge indicating the danger level. Drive through the ford slowly but steadily, and remember to dry out your brakes afterwards by applying them progressively. A careful check should be made that the road is clear ahead and behind when you do this.

Tractors

Even the best and most modern tractors move at a speed considerably lower than the average family car particularly if they are pulling a trailer.

Tractor drivers may well be oblivious of traffic approaching from behind, particularly if they are wearing ear muffs. Before passing one, signal your presence to the tractor driver with horn and headlights and, preferably, wait for some indication that he has seen

you and is aware of your intentions. You should also check that there are no turn-offs into farmyards or fields, before overtaking the tractor.

Other vehicles

Country roads provide routes for large commercial vehicles collecting or delivering produce, and huge agricultural machinery, such as combine harvesters, may be met from time to time. Due to the high

cost of combine harvesters, they are often used all round the clock at harvest time, so they could be met on the roads between fields at any time of the day or night.

Another common sight at harvest time is the fully-laden hay lorry. Hauliers tend to take on massive loads of hay, and if they are not properly secured, loose straws may whip off the lorry, or complete bales may fall on to the road.

Villages

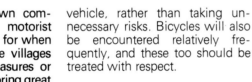

Every village has its own community life which the motorist must consider and allow for when driving through it. Some villages also contain historic treasures or beautiful settings which bring great numbers of visitors, and these too call for consideration and anticipation from the driver.

Village life

Although a village may appear to be small and quiet, it should never be forgotten that its facilities serve a wide community and it will attract a wide variety of interests. Always slow down when driving through a village, even if no speed restriction is in force.

Life in general proceeds at a slower pace than in towns. Patience should be exercised when travelling behind a slow moving vehicle, rather than taking unnecessary risks. Bicycles will also be encountered relatively frequently, and these too should be treated with respect.

One of the most common features of village life is the delivery van. In many cases, it will not be possible for the driver to park close to his destination without partially blocking the road. The driver will usually park in the best place from his own point of view, and may then walk into the road without warning. Be prepared for, and tolerant towards any inconvenience caused by this behaviour.

Country buses play an important part in rural life. They may be too large for the small lanes they have to travel down, but they usually expect, and get, priority over other traffic. Around bus stops there may be numbers of pedestrians, especially children, and they will frequently stand in the road if there is no pavement or only a small pull-in.

Another hazardous aspect of village life is the school. From 08.30 to 09.00 and from 15.00 to 16.00 as well as at lunch-time children will be coming and going to and from school. In addition to the extra traffic to be expected near a school at this time where parents collect them, also beware of children rushing into the road. Not all of them may be used to the speeds of non-local traffic.

The population that uses the village shops will probably consist of quite a high proportion of old people, very young children and people with dogs (not always on a lead). Be prepared for them.

Parking in a village calls for consideration for others. Many gateways and openings which may look unused are, in fact, in use. Parking with the wheels on the pavement may contravene local by-laws and should be avoided because of the problems it poses to pedestrians such as mothers with prams, those pushing bicycles, those with dogs on a leash, and old people.

Parking under trees may cause problems since some types of leaf exude a gum which is not only unpleasant but difficult to remove. This, as well as any flower petals and bird-droppings can damage the car's paintwork and should be washed off as soon as possible.

Remember all these possible hazards when approaching a village and reduce speed.

Village attractions

Well-known villages will attract visitors who are paying more attention to the sights than to the traffic. There may also be drivers passing through who are looking around and not at the road in front of them.

In any village with historic or scenic attractions, be prepared to find tourists. Pedestrians may suddenly walk in front of you, or the car in front could stop without warning. Coaches may also be in evidence, either parked, or trying to negotiate a narrow street. Give way to coaches whenever it is possible. If the village holds attractions for you, resist the temptation to look at them while driving through. Find a safe, clear, place to park and explore the village at leisure and on foot. Should you be visiting an historic house or monument, its car park will usually be signposted.

Local events such as a fete are very popular in the locality, and will usually be accompanied by congestion and obstruction near the entrance. Choose a different route if possible, otherwise drive with extra caution and expect problems if you intend to park close by.

The local hunt may be encountered in or near a village between November and April. It will usually be accompanied by many people on foot, intending to follow the hunt, and there may be vehicles and horse boxes parked at inconvenient places. Horses and hounds will be in a particularly excited state, so proceed with extreme caution, being prepared to stop if necessary.

Horses being ridden on the road are increasingly met in country areas. They are easily scared and you should not hoot at them or rev your engine noisily. If you cannot allow plenty of room when passing them, you should wait quietly behind them until it is clear to do so. Horses should be given priority.

Trunk roads

The fast suburban and arterial roads which link the country's towns and cities carry a wide variety of traffic whose speed and density have been increasing year by year.

Road markings

The heavily-used, fast, cross-country routes are usually well marked with advance warning of hazards, and local authorities generally erect warning signs on sharp bends. The more chevrons shown on one of these signs, the sharper will be the bend.

The lines and markings painted in the road also provide a great deal of information. In general, the more white paint that is visible on the road at any given point, the greater will be the degree of hazard there.

Centre lines

The white centre line or lines provide valuable information to the driver on the best use of the road space. A dashed line will have very short dashes if it is a lane marking, longer dashes for the centre line marking and longer still for warning line markings.

The edges of the road at bends or other hazards will be marked with a continuous white line, and with a dashed white line or no marking at all elsewhere.

Double white lines also carry an important message. Where both lines are unbroken, it is forbidden to cross them. The only exceptions to this are when a stationary vehicle is blocking the road, when a policeman or road work signals direct you across them, or to enter or leave a side road.

A broken line on one side of the solid centre line is to indicate that traffic on the side of that broken line may cross it, when overtaking, for example, provided it is safe to do so.

In some areas the two lines will spread apart, the space between being filled with diagonal solid white lines. No vehicles must drive on this area as it is there to keep traffic streams apart.

Observation

Looking well ahead when driving on trunk roads will give the driver more information as well as more time to react to it. High hedges are not common on cross-country roads, and it is usually possible to look across bends and some way into the distance to spot approaching traffic and other features, such as the next village.

Dual carriageways

Many trunk roads contain sections of dual carriageway, some of which may be wide and of almost motorway standard, and some much narrower and rather short. All dual carriageways are indicated well in advance, and a series of signs and road markings also warn when they will end.

Many dual carriageways are signed as clearways, and no parking is allowed on them at any time. Keep in the left hand lane except when overtaking, although you should not weave in and out of the lanes if there is much traffic moving slower than you are.

Turning right off dual carriageways can be a dangerous manoeuvre. You should be looking sufficiently far ahead to be able to see the turning in good time. Check the mirror and indicate as early as possible, then start to slow down in plenty of time.

Three lane roads

Considerable dangers exist on this type of road, because of the use of the centre lane for traffic going in either direction. Before entering the centre lane, whether to overtake or to turn right, take especial care that the road is clear ahead, and also for a long distance behind. Signal in good time, and keep checking the road ahead and the road behind in your mirrors.

Whenever possible, any overtaking manoeuvre on this type of road should be timed in such a way that you avoid putting your car in a 'sandwich' of the vehicle you are overtaking and a vehicle coming the other way. It is safer to wait until there is a gap in the oncoming traffic, giving yourself extra room in case any dangerous situation arises while you are overtaking.

Suburban areas

Trunk roads frequently pass through villages and small towns, and usually suburban areas. The normal life in all these places may cause problems for the motorist, but suburban areas can be particularly difficult.

A typical stretch of trunk road may pass, in a relatively short space, a shopping precinct, several industrial or business premises, schools, and housing areas. At each point, pedestrians or vehicles may suddenly cross into the path of the oncoming traffic, often without warning.

Shopping areas

Around the shopping area, cars will be found parking, often so that they partially block the road. Alternatively they may be moving off, sometimes without sufficient care or warning.

Pedestrians of all kinds, including children, elderly people, young mothers with prams and shopping, will often be trying to cross the road in these areas. If pedestrian crossings, footbridges or underpasses are not conveniently situated people will often take great risks to cross a busy road, dodging the traffic.

Around bus stops be prepared, not only for the passengers who get off and then dash from behind the bus across the road, but also for people trying to catch the bus who may appear from any direction and run across the road in front of you.

Schools

Take great care in the vicinity of schools, especially at the times they start and finish. Amber warning lights may be seen which flash at these times, and one can also expect to find a school crossing patrol helping the children to cross.

Numbers of parents, frequently with their cars, congregate around the school entrance at the start and finish times, although there are usually markings on the road which forbid parking directly in front of the school premises.

Industrial estates

Heavy goods vehicles make great use of trunk roads, often as a link between the motorway and their destination. This destination is often a factory or part of an industrial estate situated quite close to the road.

Lorries manoeuvring into and out of these areas will probably take up most of the road while they do so. Patience and consideration for the lorry drivers will be appreciated by them. The many people who work in these areas may work shift systems as well as normal working hours, so be prepared for an upsurge of pedestrian, bicycle,

motorcycle, car and bus traffic at unusual times.

Housing estates

Where the roads from a housing estate join a trunk road, one can expect to find volumes of cars trying to enter the main road, especially in the morning rush hour. The roads on housing estates have dangers of their own.

The fact that housing estates tend to be quiet during the day gives children, in particular, a false sense of security. They often play near the road, and sometimes actually on it. When chasing after something, their attention is on the object of the chase.

Frequent visitors to housing estates are ice-cream vans and mobile shops. Pedestrians, especially children, will congregate around these, and may often walk into the road without looking.

The motorway system

In 1958 when the Preston by-pass was opened, it constituted Britain's first motorway. Since then, over 1,500 miles of motorway have been constructed, providing fast, efficient and safe transport to many parts of Britain.

The usual layout of a stretch of motorway is:

Pair of hard shoulders, 10ft wide
Pair of three lane carriageways, 36ft wide
Central reservation, 13ft wide, with safety fence
Bridge clearance, 16' 6" minimum
Marker posts on both sides at 110^x intervals.
Telephone at one mile intervals opposite each other

Regulations

Motorway regulations apply from the start of motorway to the 'end of motorway' sign. The following are not allowed to use motorways:
pedestrians
learner drivers (except HGV learners)
pedal cycles
motor cycles of less than 50cc
invalid carriages (under 8cwt laden weight)
agricultural vehicles
slow moving vehicles (except by special permission)

No parking on the central reservation
No parking or reversing on the carriageways or the hard shoulder. Parking on the hard shoulder only in an emergency
No walking on the carriageways or central reservation except in an emergency. Vehicles towing trailers and those vehicles over 3 tons laden weight are not permitted to use the right hand lane except in an emergency.

Direction signs

Directional signs and route confirmatory signs are rectangular, with white lettering on a blue background. Details of these signs are given on pages 42 and 43.

Warning signs

Light signals are used to provide motorway warning signs. These are remotely-operated from the motorway control room, and are often switched on in response to a radio call from a motorway police patrol.

The operation of these signals is monitored by a computer, for safety reasons. This prevents a particular light signal from being switched on without the correct sequence of signals leading up to it also being switched on. For example, if a low speed limit is to be imposed, the computer will ensure that this is preceeded by one or more further signals, reducing the speed more gradually.

The computer also enables a continuous record to be kept of which signals were in operation, with details of the time and date. This is designed to prevent a signal from being left on inadvertently.

The signals will be found either on pedestal signs situated on the central reservation, or located on an overhead gantry. Warning signs are accompanied by amber lights flashing top and bottom. These lights do not flash for the 'all-clear' sign.

Some of these signals have red stop lights incorporated in them. These flash from side to side; when they are switched on, do not proceed any further in that lane. If these lights are located on overhead gan-

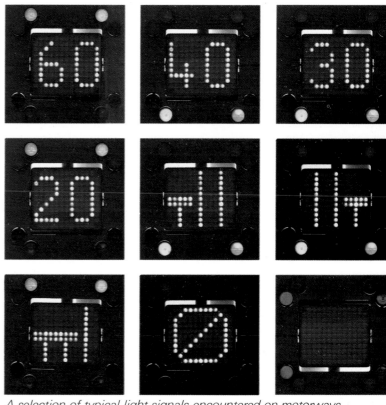

A selection of typical light signals encountered on motorways

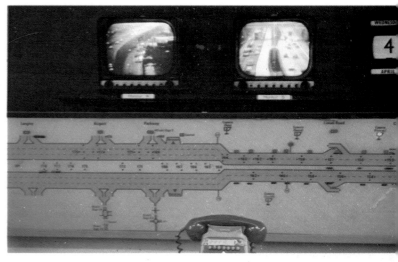

Some motorways are monitored by closed circuit television

tries, they apply only to the lane directly below them.

The earliest type of signal used was a pair of amber lights, one above the other, mounted to the left of the hard shoulder. When these flash alternately, they give warning of a hazard such as fog. Motorists are advised to slow down to 30 mph at such a signal.

Message signs

Several motorways have message signs located to the left of the hard shoulder. When not in use, these are blank, but they can be switched on to give warnings of fog, slippery road surface or an accident ahead.

Experimental signs

Some motorways have experimental light signals which are designed to convey some of the variety of information contained on the normal road warning signs.

Marker posts

These posts are placed at intervals of 110 yards on the outer edge of each hard shoulder. The sides which face the motorway bear a telephone symbol and an arrow pointing in the direction of the nearest telephone. Each post has a number accompanied by a letter A or B which indicates the carriageway concerned. No telephone is more than $\frac{1}{2}$ mile from any marker post.

Telephones

Situated one mile apart, motorway telephones are placed opposite each other, so there is never any need to cross the carriageways

Examples of motorway telephones

in order to use one. The marker posts will indicate in which direction the nearest telephone may be found.

These telephones are for use in emergencies only. They are connected to the motorway control room, and no other calls can be made from them. They are not locked and no money is needed in order to use them.

Several different styles of telephone are in use, but they all follow the same general principle. The old style telephones work only in one direction to the control room, but with the newer types, it is also possible for the control room to ring back to one of the telephones.

Breakdown

In the unfortunate event of a breakdown, it is permissible to use the hard shoulder. When stationary, the hazard warning lights should be switched on, and a warning triangle placed at least 100 yards behind the car.

Great care should be taken when getting out of the car. The driver's door should not be used as it is

so close to a carriageway of fast-moving traffic. It is preferable to get out of the car through the nearside door.

After walking to the nearest telephone, a phone call can be made to the motorway control room. The police will take details of the telephone number, the registration number, make, model, year and colour of your car, information about the breakdown, your name and address, and your membership number of a motoring organisation. They will then either ask you to ring them back, or they will ring you back to tell you what action they have taken.

If you are a member of a motoring organisation, the police pass details of the breakdown direct to them. If not, it will be necessary to pay the garage sent out by the police.

It is unwise to leave your car on the hard shoulder for more than a few hours. It is a very hazardous position, and the police move vehicles left in such a place as quickly as possible, charging the owners for doing so. They will also remove your car if you have been involved in a collision or are blocking a carriageway.

Joining and leaving the motorway

Joining the motorway

The entry onto a motorway is made along a two-lane slip road which leads into an acceleration lane. Some slip roads have tight corners, so do not speed up too quickly, but do not hesitate either. As you drive down the slip road watch the traffic in the nearside lane of the motorway, looking for gaps. Long before you reach the point of merging with it, check the mirrors

and switch on the right indicators. Look over your right shoulder for gaps in the traffic and match your speed to that of the other vehicles. When a suitable gap occurs, move smoothly into the nearside lane, and cancel the right indicators.

Should traffic on the motorway be so dense that you reach the end of the slip road before a suitable gap has presented itself you must be prepared to stop. You should not try to force your way into the traffic stream, nor should you drive on the hard shoulder.

Once safely on the motorway, accustom yourself to motorway speeds before building up to your desired cruising speed.

When overtaking watch carefully for traffic approaching from behind. It may well be going faster than you think.

Leaving the motorway

On the approach to a junction where you intend to turn off, check the mirrors, switch on the left indicators and move into the nearside lane as early as possible, between the half-mile signpost and the 300 yard countdown sign.

The adjustment from motorway speeds to the halt likely to be required at the junction roundabout needs to take place over a

relatively short distance. It is better to glance at the speedometer once or twice on the exit slip road than to rely on one's subjective assessment of speed. Even after joining the subsequent non-motorway road, check your speed from time to time, as it takes a short while to recover from the rhythm of high speed motorway driving and adapt to the slower speeds of other roads.

Direction signs

The approach to the motorway is marked by the international symbol for a motorway, together with its number. From this point until the end of the motorway, all motorway regulations apply. A similar sign crossed diagonally with a red bar indicates the end of a motorway and all its regulations.

One mile from each junction, the direction sign shows the junction number and also the number of the most important road number leading away from that junction.

The sign at half a mile from the junction repeats the junction number and gives more information including some of the main destinations reached.

Service areas

Signs indicating service areas are placed one mile before the turn-off. In some areas there are long distances between service areas, and it is preferable to stop at the first convenient one, particularly if you have been driving continuously for over two hours, rather than continue to the next service area.

The approach to a service area needs great care. The precise layout of the parking areas and roads to the fuel pumps will not be clear until the last moment. In the car park vehicles and pedestrians will be moving in all directions. You will need to lose almost all your speed on the approach

slip road, so that you are not going too fast when you enter the car park. Because it is difficult to adjust quickly from the high motorway speeds to the much lower ones required in a service area use your speedometer to get an idea of your speed, rather than rely on your subjective impressions.

From time to time, traffic may have to be diverted off a section of the motorway, to return to it farther along its length. The cause may be roadworks or an accident. A system of signs has been devised in which the diversion route is indicated by a geometric symbol in yellow with a black border.

To keep to a diversion route, all that is necessary is to follow the yellow and black symbols wherever they appear.

The start of the deceleration lane leading to the exit slip road is prefaced by countdown markers at distances of 300 yards, 200 yards and 100 yards.

The slip road itself has a confirmatory direction sign, repeating the junction number, the details of the roads and the destinations reached from that junction.

Road markings on the approach to a junction include large arrows indicating the start of the deceleration lane. That lane is bounded by a dashed white line incorporating green reflective markers. Some junctions also have the junction number painted on the motorway at the approach.

Junctions in urban areas, or where motorways merge and separate are usually heralded by gantry signs. These contain the junction number, direction information relevant to the lanes below them. They also frequently carry flashing light signals, and are sometimes found at distances of $\frac{2}{3}$ mile and $\frac{1}{3}$ mile from the junction.

Motorway driving

Motorways have a better safety record than other roads, and provide fast communication links over long distances. Their freedom from interruptions such as roundabouts, traffic lights and sharp bends means that uninterrupted travel is possible for long distances. Large volumes of traffic can be carried provided everyone observes good lane discipline. Long distances on motorways can prove monotonous, so regular breaks for refreshment and exercise should be taken.

When preparing your car for a motorway journey be sure to check tyres, petrol, oil and water

Car preparation

The strains on a car during a motorway journey can be greater than on other journeys because of the higher continuous speeds involved and the longer distances. A breakdown can be an expensive annoyance on a motorway, and reliability is essential.

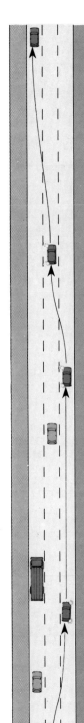

Lane discipline

This is one of the most crucial aspects of motorway driving. A common but dangerous misconception is that the right hand lane, especially on three lane motorways, is a 'fast' lane. This is not the case, it is an overtaking lane only and is not to be used for continuous motoring at 70 mph.

The left hand lane should normally be used on two and three lane carriageways. Occasionally it is filled with slow, heavy traffic, for example on some hills.

The centre lane (or right hand lane where there are only two) is used for overtaking the traffic in the left hand lane. Where there is a stream of slower traffic in the left hand lane, however, it may be preferable to remain in the centre lane until all the vehicles have been passed, rather than weaving in and out of the lanes. As soon as possible, however, return to the left hand lane. Do not stay in the centre lane if the left hand lane is empty.

All lane changes need to be planned well in advance because of the speeds involved. Always look well ahead so that the need to overtake another vehicle is realised in good time. Carefully check in your mirrors for any traffic approaching from behind. Keep checking this during the overtaking manoeuvre as it is easy to underestimate the speed of following traffic.

Braking distances

A consequence of the fact that speeds are higher on motorways is that braking distances will be greater. It is not always realised just how great these distances become. At 70 mph on a dry road with tyres, car, and driver in first class condition, it takes over 300 feet to stop completely. This is equivalent to about 23 car lengths.

If the roads are wet, the tyres are worn, or the driver's reactions are slow, this distance becomes more than 600 feet, or 46 car lengths. These very long braking distances serve to emphasise the importance of adequate spacing between vehicles on motorways.

Consideration for others

Always try not to baulk other vehicles when driving on a motorway. Before beginning any overtaking manoeuvre, consider whether your car's acceleration is fast enough to take you past the vehicle in front and back into the nearside lane without holding up other, faster traffic wishing to overtake you.

When approaching a motorway junction it is frequently possible to see traffic travelling along the approach slip road intending to join the motorway. It makes their entry on to the motorway simpler if you move from the left hand lane to the centre lane (having checked the mirrors and signalled correctly well before reaching them.

Lorry drivers are grateful for consideration on motorways. Heavy goods vehicles are forbidden to use the right hand lane on a three lane motorway, and must make the best progress they can on the other two lanes. These heavy vehicles sometimes have a separate 'crawler' lane reserved for them on hills. Cars towing caravans are also banned from using the right hand lane on three lane motorways.

Night driving

Dipped headlights should generally be used when travelling on motorways. In spite of the distance between carriageways, it is still possible to dazzle oncoming motorists if main beam lights are used. Always dip your lights if the possibility of dazzle exists.

The system of reflective studs used on motorways is red for the left hand side, with green at junctions, white along lane markings and amber on the right hand side.

Adverse weather

Whenever visibility is restricted by the weather, switch on dipped headlights and high-intensity rear lights. Even when it is not actually raining, the spray thrown up by motorway traffic from a wet road can reduce visibility considerably.

In heavy rain; it is especially important that speeds should be considerably reduced as visibility will be low and braking distances will be increased. (See pages 62–65).

In fog take especial care. Drive slowly so that you could stop in the distance you can see to be clear. Do not be tempted to speed up in order to keep in sight of the lights of the vehicle in front. Do not also be tempted to believe the fog is thinner than it actually is.

The fog immediately behind a vehicle often looks thinner, but this will be found to be a false impression should you try to overtake. Keep watching your speed and always obey any speed restriction signs. It is easy to unwittingly allow speed to build up to a dangerously high level. (See pages 70–73).

Light snow does not usually block motorways altogether, although it may result in at least one lane being impassable.

Motorways are particularly susceptible to cross-winds. Keep a sharp look out for any stretches which seem as though they may be badly affected, and keep firm steering control of the car when passing high-sided vehicles. (See pages 66–67).

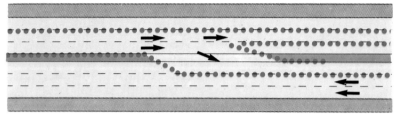

Extensive roadworks schemes can involve directing some traffic on to the opposite carriageway. These changes are given plenty of warning and the correct lane should be selected early

Roadworks

Most motorways are subject at one time or another to maintenance or improvement works. These can sometimes be substantial undertakings lasting for years.

All roadworks are preceded by sets of warning signs and, sometimes, flashing light signals. In nearly every case high speeds are impossible past roadworks, so you should slow down as soon as the first indication of roadworks is displayed.

When the roadworks are extensive, some lanes of the motorway may be switched on to the other carriageway. This sometimes means you have to make an early decision about the junction at which you need to leave the motorway, since that particular stream may be separated some miles before the junction. This emphasises the importance of planning your route so that you know which junction number you need to take in order to leave the motorway.

Fatigue

Driving for long distances on motorways can be monotonous, and it can lead to drowsiness and fatigue. Try to prevent this from happening by keeping the car well-ventilated, listening to the radio occasionally, checking instruments regularly, and constantly shifting your gaze.

Avoiding heavy meals before or during a journey will lessen the chances of fatigue setting in, as will taking regular breaks, at least every three hours, and more often if you feel like it.

Should you feel yourself becoming drowsy, you should realise that you cannot stop on the hard shoulder and sleep. Get off the motorway at the next exit, however, or at the first service area. Park the car in a safe place off the road, and either sleep there, or take a few minutes' break with some brisk exercise to get the blood circulating again. (See pages 92 and 93).

Speed limits should always be obeyed, particularly in bad weather.

Town driving

The majority of motorists spend a large proportion of their time driving in traffic and usually experience some congestion. These delays can be the cause of great irritation among drivers, with a consequent lowering of driving standards.

Driving attitudes

Observation and anticipation of events around you will give time to plan your driving well ahead and to execute the necessary moves without having to interrupt the traffic flow.

Courtesy to other drivers can calm ruffled tempers as well as smooth the traffic flow. Allowing some traffic from a side road to join the main traffic stream will relieve congestion without delaying you a great deal. A sensible system for this kind of situation is for one car from the side road to fit in front of one car in the main stream, the second in front of the one behind, and so on.

A relaxed attitude to the journey will make it considerably pleasanter for you, and probably for other drivers as well. This can be brought about by planning the journey so that you know exactly where to go, and have arranged matters so that you have plenty of time to complete it. Starting earlier or delaying the intended time of arrival will usually help you feel more relaxed. Try to avoid rush hour travel which so greatly increases fuel consumption at slow speed. Try to curb your impatience over other drivers' mistakes or bad driving. Give them enough room to sort themselves out rather than trying to compete with them or forcing them to conform to your own ideas.

Traffic lights

Look well ahead for traffic lights, particularly those with filter lanes. Always try to get into the right lane for your destination as early as possible. A late lane change may be impossible without severely inconveniencing the other traffic and risking an accident. If you find yourself in the wrong lane and cannot easily move to the right one, it will be necessary to continue in the wrong direction until you have an opportunity to turn off, return and try again.

The intention to turn right should be signalled and the move made to the right-turning lane as early as possible. At traffic lights keep the right indicators going for the information of the other traffic. Never leave it until the last minute before switching them on.

Always try to avoid making any congestion worse. At traffic lights in heavy traffic, for example, even if the lights are green, do not cross the junction unless you can see the exit is clear.

In some towns the traffic lights are linked to allow heavy traffic to flow at a steady speed.

All traffic must turn left

Box junctions

A box of yellow crossed lines marked on the road at a junction defines an area which no one should enter unless they can see it is clear on the far side. This practice should always be carried out at junctions, whether marked with a yellow box or not, but where the box is in place it is an offence to block it.

The one exception to this regulation is for drivers intending to turn right. If the road into which they intend to move is clear, it is permissible to wait in the box junction for a gap in the opposing traffic. More than one vehicle intending to turn right may wait in a line (but not a whole column), provided oncoming traffic wishing to turn right is not blocked thereby.

Right turns are banned here

One-way streets

Modern traffic schemes make increasing use of one-way streets in order to speed up traffic flow. Those unfamiliar with town driving may find themselves in situations where the presence or not of a one-way street is uncertain.

When joining a one-way street from a side road, a one-way sign will indicate the direction of traffic flow. If this is obscured, perhaps by a parked van, it is not always easy to tell that it is in fact, a one-way street. A hint is given by the fact that all the parked vehicles will be facing one way. Vehicles are normally parked facing the same direction as the traffic flow.

One-way street lane markings

Lane discipline in a one-way street is important. Select the lane which will lead to your destination, using either lane markings or direction signs for information, then stay in it. A right hand or left hand lane is preferable to a centre lane, however, because traffic is entitled to overtake on either side in a one-way street.

Side streets leading off the one-way street may also be one-way. You should expect traffic to join the street from either side, and if you are intending to turn off down a side-street, look well ahead to confirm that entry to it is actually allowed. The confusion caused by making a mistake about this can be dangerous.

Bus lanes are sometimes laid down in one-way streets. The correct use of these is explained on pages 48 and 49. The use of contra-flow bus lanes in one-way streets may cause confusion when the situation is first encountered. Look out for the warning signs, and take care not to stray into the bus lane.

Tidal flow traffic working

Some wide two-way streets are adapted for tidal flow traffic working to help avoid peak-time delays.

Light signals on gantries across the road indicate by an arrow or a red cross the direction of flow along each lane. Where a red cross shows you should move out of that lane, as it will be open to traffic from the opposite direction.

Tidal flow lane indicators

Town driving

The task of driving safely in towns is eased by an intelligent anticipation of the behaviour of other road users. Traffic in towns may become very congested, but every driver can minimise his own contribution to any congestion by driving smoothly, and with courtesy and consideration.

Pedestrians

In a busy street pedestrians may spill off the pavement into the road, so you should never drive so close to the kerb that they may be struck by door handles or wing mirrors for example.

An important situation in which to check for pedestrians is when turning left or right. Many people walk across side roads without looking, assuming the traffic on the main road will continue straight on. A gentle sound on the horn will tell them you are there, but remember that the pedestrian has priority and also that some people are deaf.

Pedestrian crossings

Pedestrians have the right of way on these crossings and traffic must stop for them. Drivers should stop at the give way line placed about one yard from the crossing. Within the area defined by the zig-zag road markings, no parking or overtaking is allowed. Some zebra crossings are divided into two parts by a central island.

Look out for pedestrian crossings well ahead of you. This will give plenty of time to slow down gently for any pedestrians, either on the crossing or waiting to cross. Children and old people should be given plenty of time to cross. In heavy traffic, do not stop on the crossing itself, but wait until there is enough space on the other side.

Pelican crossings are controlled by traffic lights activated by the pedestrians. These lights incorporate an amber flashing light, which authorises traffic to proceed only if there is no one on the crossing.

When the amber light flashes . . .

Stop at the Pelican crossing

Cyclists

Cyclists have a particularly difficult time in town traffic, and they should be given plenty of room. They may appear unexpectedly between you and the kerb, and you should always check for them along the nearside before turning left.

On a windy day in a city street, gusts of wind will blow between the buildings, and these could easily blow a cyclist out into the road. A cyclist who looks round and behind him is very likely to turn across your path.

Some towns have set aside reserved lanes for cyclists, where motorists are not allowed to drive.

Motor cyclists

Like cyclists, motor cyclists may also appear unexpectedly, and you should look out for them when turning and at junctions.

Although they are not so easily seen, and sometimes do not use their headlights in towns, they are just as fast as other vehicles and may well be weaving their way quickly through the traffic.

Buses

Wherever you are, always find out if you are on a bus route. In towns most of the busy roads will be bus routes and you should look well ahead to spot the bus stops.

Always give way to buses, provided it is safe to do so, particularly when they are pulling away from a bus stop. In the vicinity of a bus stop be prepared for bus passengers to jump off the bus just before it comes to a halt, and for people crossing the road behind and in front of the bus.

Take extra care near bus stops

When passing a bus at a bus stop check whether there is any movement of its wheels. If this is very slight it is probably safe to pass with caution, but otherwise it is better to let the bus go first.

Bus lanes

In some towns special lanes have been marked out and set aside for the use of buses. They may sometimes also be used by taxis. Signs at the start of the lane indicate which times of the day these lanes operate. These may be during peak hours, or the lane may be in continuous use for 24 hours. During their use, all vehicles are prohibited from driving or parking in them. They may be crossed when turning right or left, although this must be done with great care.

The bus lane may sometimes go in the opposite direction to the traffic in a one-way street.

Contra-flow bus lane

Taxis

In large cities taxis make up a substantial part of the traffic. They are very manoeuvrable and often drive fast. When picking up or setting down fares they are liable to stop suddenly, or to swing right across the road. You should allow room for the taxi to move or stop unexpectedly, without having to brake harshly yourself.

Delivery vans may double park and cause obstruction

Other vehicle hazards

Delivery vans and milk floats may cause a hazard to the unwary by stopping unexpectedly or blocking the road. Good observation and anticipation should prevent anyone being baulked by them.

The sound of a siren or klaxon warns everyone of the presence of a police car, fire engine or ambulance. If you cannot see a flashing blue light or headlights in front of you, this vehicle is probably approaching from behind or from the side. You should pull well to the side as soon as possible and stop until it has passed. Remember that one emergency vehicle may be closely followed by another, so make sure it is safe before starting off again.

Special consideration should be given to cars carrying L-plates. If the car belongs to a driving school, it is very likely there will be a novice behind the wheel.

49

Parking

Parking, especially in the larger cities, is often so restricted that motorists can spend a large amount of time searching for a space. A variety of different parking control systems is in use, and familiarity with all of them will make life easier and may avoid a parking fine.

Road signs and markings

The general sign indicating the existence of waiting restrictions is circular, with a blue background, a border and a single red bar diagonally across it. Beyond this sign, different restrictions will apply in different areas. The precise details of these restrictions are provided by kerbside signs and yellow lines and markings on the kerb.

Double yellow lines mean that no waiting is allowed (except for loading and unloading) during any working day and at times outside normal working hours.

The yellow sign mounted on the post at the kerbside gives more details of what these times are. It may be a continuous restriction which applies on every day including Sundays and Bank Holidays, or a shorter period.

A single yellow line restricts waiting during every working day, and again, the details of the times when this is in force are given on the kerbside sign.

A dashed yellow line restricts waiting for periods shorter than the working day, details being provided by the kerbside signs.

Restrictions on loading and unloading may be applied in addition to the yellow lines, which do not in themselves limit the loading or unloading period. Three yellow stripes marked on the kerb or the edge of the carriageway mean no loading or unloading for a period longer than any working day.

A white sign on a kerbside post details this more precisely, and it may extend to no loading and unloading at any time.

Two yellow stripes mean no loading and unloading during any working day. Single yellow stripes reduce this restriction to a period shorter than any working day.

Roadside parking areas

Areas of some streets in towns and cities are sometimes set aside for limited short-term free parking. Notices near them detail the period allowed, and they also generally forbid return within a specified time. Some of these roadside parking areas are reserved for the exclusive use of local residents.

Parking meters

Many places charge motorists for parking space on the street by the use of parking meters.

A certain amount of parking time can be bought for a given payment. The rate can vary considerably from one town or area to another,

but is always given on a plate fixed to the side of the meter.

Normally, insertion of the appropriate coin operates the mechanism, but with some types it is necessary to turn a lever as well. You are at liberty to take advantage of any unexpired time remaining on an unoccupied meter.

Where you find the meter does not work, you should attach a note to it stating the fact. You may then park at that spot for the maximum time available on that meter.

A parking meter covered with a transparent plastic bag is one which the traffic warden has discovered as inoperative. All of these and any other meters which do not work are regularly repaired by a

parking meter mechanic.

When the meter has been repaired he will set it to the maximum time available on the meter. Any vehicle remaining there after expiry of that time will be liable to get a parking ticket and may be towed away by the police. Fines imposed for overstaying time at a meter are reviewed constantly and are increased periodically.

Occasionally, a meter may be covered by a red hood. This is the equivalent of converting it to a no-waiting sign, and is an indication that the area must be kept clear. Any vehicle parked there is very likely to be towed away, and the driver charged the recovery fee as well as the fine for illegal parking at that bay.

Pay-and-display car parks

Off-the-road parking is often provided in open-air car parks where certain defined periods of parking time can be bought.

The ticket supplied by the meter in exchange for the correct money must be fixed to one of the car windows, and be visible to the car park attendant. Failure to display a ticket can lead to a parking fine.

Multi-storey car parks

A multi-storey car park is often the most convenient place to park, although these parks are, generally, fairly expensive.

Upon entry to the car park a ticket is issued stating the time and date. When you leave the car take this ticket with you.

Parking techniques

In a car park, it is simpler and saves petrol to reverse into a parking space. The manoeuvring necessary is best done when the engine is warm. When starting from cold, the car can move forward with no interruption, thereby saving fuel. It is also often easier to manoeuvre precisely when driving in reverse. To save possible damage to your car you should park as centrally and as far back as possible in a parking space.

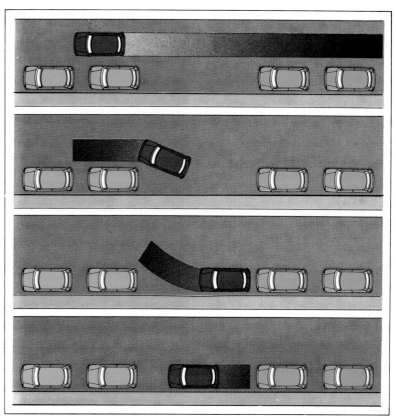

Parking parallel with the kerb is a manoeuvre which many people are hesitant about and consequently avoid. The technique is as follows:

Drive alongside and stop parallel with the vehicle in front of the space in which you intend to park.

Check your mirrors and indicate left (if you are on the left side of the road). When it is safe to do so, reverse very slowly with only slight left lock until your rear wheels are in a line with the rear of that vehicle.

Increase left lock, looking at the far corner of the parking space.

Continue slowly until your front wheels are in a line with the rear of the vehicle in front.

Watching the front of your car now, straighten up until the front nearside corner is past the rear bumper of the vehicle in front.

From this point, watch the rear of your car again, and apply full right lock.

Continue slowly until your car is close to the vehicle behind and is parallel to the kerb.

Drive slowly forwards, straightening up, to position your car midway between the other vehicles.

Road surfaces

Most roads in Britain and Western Europe have a permanent covering on them. It is usually either white-topped (concrete cast as a continuous ribbon or in slabs) or black-topped (asphalt-covered). To counteract the effects of frost, ice and snow, many Alpine roads, and some roads in Holland, have stone blocks or even hard brick surfaces, which give a reasonable grip with good drainage.

Stone chips

Black-topped roads usually have small stone chips rolled into them in order to improve their grip under all weather conditions. The asphalt binds these stones, and acts as a cushion, spreading some of the load. The stones take the abrasive wear and crushing loads of the passing traffic.

Because they are generally quarried locally, the stone chips vary in their 'grippiness' from one part of the country to another. The granite chips of the Grampians, for example, are hard, durable, resistant to traffic polish, and give an extremely good wet grip. The gravel stones found near London and the Home Counties give a lower friction grip, are softer and therefore polish more readily, and tend to give less of that distinctive tyre rumble. Economics, however,

guide Local Authorities as to which chips they use, subject to laid-down standards of evenness and surface-grip.

Special surfaces

In a few accident black spot areas, and where the density of heavy goods traffic warrants it, special surface dressings are applied, which give remarkable polish resistance, very good wet grip, and a low maintenance cost. The

materials are scientifically designed, and initially more costly, using graded stones and special materials to obtain the desired qualities.

On some elevated sections of roads, where black ice could be a danger, the roadway has electric wires embedded in it. These can be switched on to prevent ice forming, or to melt light snow deposits.

Newly surfaced roads

If the new surface on a road has not hardened, drive slowly over it. The excess stones can be flung up by your own vehicle, as well as by those in front, overtaking or passing in the opposite direction. They can chip off paint, scratch glass and even shatter windscreens. The tar picked up on your tyres is harmful to rubber, but never remove it with a rag dipped in solvent such as petrol, paraffin or

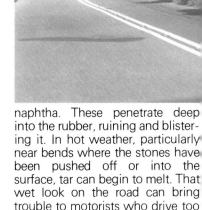

naphtha. These penetrate deep into the rubber, ruining and blistering it. In hot weather, particularly near bends where the stones have been pushed off or into the surface, tar can begin to melt. That wet look on the road can bring trouble to motorists who drive too fast into the bend or brake hard. Tyre grip is reduced and the surface is easily formed into ridges.

Potholes

Badly-maintained roads with deep potholes should be negotiated at a relatively slow speed, dipping into and out of each pothole, and steering round the worst of them. Those with greater experience of rough roads may prefer to drive at a speed high enough for the wheels to bounce from the rim of one pothole to the next.

Camber

Most roads have a certain amount of camber to give rapid drainage of the surface water. By introducing a controlled amount of texture roughness to both white-top and black-top surfaces, more drainage channels can be introduced to cope with heavy rainfall.

A change of camber as the road bends can have a marked effect on the car's handling. The steering response is governed by the design and layout of suspension and tyres, in relation to the weight distribution of the car. Depending on the tyre-to-road-grip, the nature of the road surface, and the radius of the bend, there is a certain speed for every car above which it will drift out tangentially on a given bend. Whereas it may be just safe to enter and exit a given bend at 50 mph in good conditions, a summer shower may bring the speed down to 30 mph, and black ice could reduce it to 15 mph.

Surface damage

The most important function of a road is its ability to take the crushing forces exerted by the traffic passing over it. A heavily loaded rolling tyre tends to 'flow' the road surface ahead and to the side of it.

The fact that the track of the wheels does not vary a great deal from one truck or bus to another means that a rhythmic pattern of ripples develop in the road surface, leading to eventual collapse.

This is most pronounced at the

approaches to traffic lights, inter-sections, roundabouts, or any section of road where inclines cause drivers to shift into lower gears. The loads tend to oscillate on the springs, particularly when braking or taking up a lower gear.

This rabbit-like pounding of the road can result in substantial road deformation. The greater the traffic density and the axle loading, the greater is the resultant damage.

Are you a better driver?

Do you think you are a good driver? It is very likely that you are interested in driving, otherwise you would not be reading this book. It is also likely that you will be a good driver. There is a difference, however, between being a good driver and being a better driver. This is not necessarily a question of your own belief in your abilities, but it is rather more a matter of how you behave towards other road users and how safely you handle unexpected situations.

The questions on this spread should set you thinking about your driving. Try to answer as you honestly believe you would have behaved in the situation described, not as you think you ought to have done with hindsight! The answers to the questions are also given on this spread but do not read them until you have answered the questions. They can easily be covered over with a piece of paper while you record your answers.

1 You realise you have just missed a right turning you had intended to take. Do you:
a take the next convenient turning on the right, reverse into the main road, then return to your intended turning?

b stop just past the first convenient left turning, reverse into it, then turn right, back into the main road, and continue to your originally intended turning?
c carry out a U-turn in the main road as soon as it is safe to do so and return to the turning?

2 You are approaching a T-junction with a major road. It is marked with double broken white lines across its mouth. There is no traffic on the major road. Are you obliged to stop before turning into it?
a Yes
b No

3 You are driving round a right hand bend. The road surface is dry and traffic is light. For maximum stability should you:
a keep your speed constant throughout the bend, leaving it at the same speed that you entered it?
b take your foot off the throttle and be prepared to brake if your speed gets too high?
c use light throttle and aim to leave the bend slightly faster than you entered it?

4 You are planning to overtake a lorry on a stretch of dual carriageway. Before starting the manoeuvre should you:
a switch on your right indicators, then check in your mirrors that all is clear behind before starting to overtake?
b check your mirrors before you switch on your right indicators?

5 You are driving along a narrow road with a constant stream of opposing traffic. Suddenly, a car turns out from the left and is proceeding directly in front of you. Your speed is such that you must slow down rapidly to avoid hitting him. Do you:
a change down through the gears as quickly as you can?
b brake hard, then release the brakes, then brake hard again?
c brake hard only once, keeping the brakes on all the time?

6 You are approaching a set of traffic lights which are at red. You are still some distance away from them and can see a small queue of traffic waiting at them. Do you:
a ease off the power to slow the car gently, waiting for the lights to change before you get there?
b change into third gear when you get nearer to the lights?
c brake early so that you can accelerate when the lights change?

7 You are driving along a motorway in light traffic. You are in the right hand lane and have just completed overtaking a vehicle in the centre lane. You are about to begin your return to the centre lane when you notice another car has approached very rapidly from behind, and appears to be planning to overtake you on the inside. Do you:

a move as quickly as you can into the centre lane so that he will be able to pass you without breaking the law?

b stay where you are for the time being, allowing him to carry out the dangerous and illegal manoeuvre of overtaking on the wrong side?

8 You are driving in a small town approaching a section of road with cars parked on both sides. The road is effectively wide enough for only one vehicle. At the far end of the line of parked cars, another car appears and flashes his headlights. Do you:

a accept his invitation to come on and drive forward immediately?

b stop and wait to see what he does next before placing any interpretation on his signal?

c invite the other driver to come on by flashing your headlights at him?

Answers

1 a Reversing from a side road into a main road is dangerous and should never be done.
b Correct. Make sure the left side road is clear by looking into it as you drive past, preparatory to reversing into it.
c Carrying out a U-turn can be dangerous, particularly if there is much traffic on the main road.

2 a The broken white double lines mean 'Give Way'. There may also be a 'Give Way' sign or a white inverted triangle marked on the road. This means that you should give way to any traffic on the major road, but that if it is clear you may proceed.
b Correct.

3 a You should get your speed right on the approach to a bend, braking or changing gear if necessary. Taking the bend on a trailing throttle does not give you adequate control or the car maximum stability.

b Your speed should never become too high during a bend if you have assessed it correctly during the approach and slowed if necessary before reaching the bend. You should not take your foot off the throttle, as applying the power helps to give the car stability. Never brake on a bend unless in an emergency and even then do not brake any more harshly than necessary. The tyres, already under cornering forces, may skid.
c Correct. Progressive throttle through the bend increases the car's stability, although the amount of power should be carefully controlled. Once you can see that the exit of the bend is clear, accelerate smoothly, but not too harshly, out of it.

4 a Switching on your right indicators denotes your intention to move to the right. You should have checked in your mirrors that it was safe to do so before indicating your intention to overtake.
b Correct. Once you have decided on your course of action, you should always check in your mirrors before making a signal of any kind.

5 a You should never attempt to slow down suddenly or in an emergency using the gears.

Precious seconds will be lost while the clutch is disengaged and you are changing gear. During this time, no speed will be lost. The brakes are designed to stop the car and should be used for this purpose.
b Correct. This technique of releasing the brakes just before they lock up then quickly re-applying them is the safest way to stop, particularly if the road surface is poor or slippery. The process is repeated as often as necessary to stop the car. You should have spotted the side turning earlier, however, and been prepared for a vehicle to emerge.
c Keeping the brakes hard on could easily lead to the wheels locking up and a resulting skid.

6 a Correct. By looking ahead you will have seen the red traffic lights in good time. You will conserve fuel by staying in top gear for as long as possible.
b Changing gear nearer the lights is unnecessary and wasteful. If you need to slow down nearer the lights, use the brakes.
c Braking now will slow you down more than necessary and the subsequent burst of acceleration will waste fuel.

7 a Changing lanes quickly could be very dangerous. If the other car is moving very fast, he could well have committed himself to overtaking you on the inside before you move, and to do so would be to risk a collision. You should never try to force another driver to do what you want him to do, even if you are trying to stop him breaking the law.
b Correct. If the other driver is intent on breaking the law you should not do anything dangerous to try to stop him.

8 a You would be foolish to automatically assume the other driver's flash on his headlmaps was an invitation to come on. He could have meant the opposite, that he intended to "come on". Headlamp signals are very ambiguous and can be easily misinterpreted. The only safe meaning they can have is I am here.
b Correct. You should not assume the other driver's headlamp flash was an invitation until it is confirmed or otherwise by what he does next.
c You should never flash your own lights to convey a signal or a message to another driver.

Winter driving

Bright sunlight

Although bright sunlight is generally welcome, it can bring problems of visibility to the motorist. The human eye is extremely adaptable to a wide range of light intensities, much more so than a camera, but it cannot see comfortably in very intense light or dazzle.

The eye

The normal human eye can see all the colours from violet to red in the visible spectrum, but not ultra-violet or infra-red rays. It can cope with quite high intensities of light, but staring directly at the sun for any length of time can permanently damage the retina and cause a partial or total blindness.

The very bright light reflected from snow on mountain tops can also affect the eye, although not permanently. It may be the cause of the painful external inflammation, conjunctivitis.

Wet roads can cause serious dazzle problems

Windscreen glass

The glass of the windscreen and the other windows absorbs 20% of the light passing through it if it is clean (more if it is dirty). For this reason, if for no other, that part of the windscreen which the eyes regularly look through should be not tinted at all. Night driving, in particular, will be made more difficult. The driver is better advised to use sunglasses in bright sunlight, which can then be removed when visibility is reduced.

The main value of tinting the upper part of the windscreen is in keeping down the temperature of the car interior a little.

Dazzle

Intensely bright spots or shafts of light, such as headlight beams, bright sunlight or reflections off water, can cause dazzle. The pupil reacts quickly, but not instantaneously and there may be a temporary 'blinding' which is a serious hazard. All the softer colours and the objects in partial shade temporarily disappear and contours become indistinct. For the average person in good health, however, the eye makes a partial recovery in a second or so. During the short period of 'blindness' the driver must rely on what he has memorised of the scene ahead and to the side.

The reflected light which causes dazzle is particularly disturbing because it becomes partly or wholly polarised. The eye is extremely sensitive to this polarised light.

A few people, however, suffer from the effects of excessive brightness (photo-phobia).

Sherry-brown tinted sunglasses

Green tinted sunglasses absorb some infra-red light

Sunglasses

Some people manage to drive in bright light without wearing sunglasses. If there are no unpleasant side effects such as headaches, soreness or watering of the eyes, there is probably no need to wear them.

The use of sunglasses when driving at night, in order to avoid dazzle from oncoming headlights is extremely ill-advised for it reduces your ability to pick out poorly-lit objects. In Germany it is illegal to drive at night with glasses of anything more than 15% absorption.

When considering the range of sunglasses available, choose a pair with good lenses. Any waviness on the surface (detected by watching through them something with straight lines, such

as a building, then moving the lenses up and down and from left to right), or prismatic effects (detected by looking through the lens at a fixed point, then rotating the lens round that point, when no movement should be seen) will produce symptoms of fatigue and headaches while driving.

Plastic lenses can be a false economy because some types scratch so easily.

Three basic types of sunglasses are in common use.

Tinted

Deeply-tinted lenses are available to cut down visible and ultra-violet light, and, in some cases, infra-red as well. The colour of the tint is important. Sherry-brown or grey tints are best for preserving colour neutrality, but some green

Photochromic lenses

Polarised lenses

or darker element is necessary to absorb infra-red. Good sunglasses should cut out about 75% of the infra-red radiation.

The better quality sunglasses of this type will bear an indication of the amount of light they absorb. A higher absorption figure, perhaps 85%, may be preferable for tropical wear, use at sea or in high mountains. The general rule is to choose the lightest tint which gives comfortable protection.

Some eye defects aggravate the discomfort caused by sunshine. If you suffer discomfort, even when wearing sunglasses, it is wiser to have your eyes checked, rather than try out darker lenses.

Photochromic

These lenses automatically darken in bright light, and lighten in poor sunlight. They are also affected by the temperature, darkening in low temperatures and lightening in warm ones.

An important factor with this type of lens is the time it takes to darken fully, and, especially, the recovery time (the time to return to the lightest state). The recovery time is longer than the time taken to darken, and this can cause problems when driving in rapidly changing light intensity.

Polarised

This type of lens is particularly effective against the dazzle and glare of light reflected off wet surfaces. No colour distortion is caused, although the overall light reduction is usually less than with other types of sunglasses. They show up the stress pattern on toughened-glass windscreens.

Winter sun

The winter sun brings problems of its own. For most of the day, sunglasses are rarely required, but the effect of driving into the slanting rays of the sun when it is low in the sky is irritating.

Photochromic glasses are less effective in these circumstances. The low ultra-violet content of the sun's rays, combined with the warm temperature of the car's interior, mean that this type of lens may not darken sufficiently. Lowering the sun visor often cuts down the rays adequately but it reduces your field of vision.

A better solution to this problem is to keep a pair of fixed tint sunglasses of, say, 65% absorption in the car and to put them on when you are driving into the setting sun.

Tunnels

The switch from bright light to relative darkness on entering a tunnel causes a potentially dangerous situation. Photochromic sunglasses will not lighten quickly enough; and fixed-tint sunglasses will not lighten at all, of course. If you wear sunglasses when entering a tunnel you will be unable to see for the first few yards. The best solution is to remove any sunglasses before entering the tunnel.

When driving in Europe, a series of short tunnels may have to be negotiated. They often have two lanes in either direction and can have a bend in the middle. Always switch on headlights so that you can see and be seen, even if the tunnel has overhead lighting.

Never change lanes when driving in a tunnel, and do not drive too fast. If you are in any doubt about the tunnel and exit layout, reduce speed gradually. Do not brake sharply or drive very slowly, for the car behind may not have seen you in time and could drive into you.

Slanting sunlight through an avenue of trees requires careful concentration

59

Night driving

Amber and blue street lighting produce different effects, particularly on colours

In some circumstances driving at night can be easier than daylight driving. The roads may be clearer of traffic and you can sometimes see approaching vehicles from a greater distance. On the other hand, however, the dazzle from oncoming headlights can be unpleasant and even dangerous. The golden rule is always to drive at such a speed that you can stop within the distance your headlights show to be clear.

Always look carefully into dark areas between street lights

Eyes at night

The eyes react to dim light and darkness by opening the pupil wide. Adaptation from bright light to relative darkness takes several seconds, and some people take longer than others to adapt. Prolonged bouts of cigarette smoking can increase the adaptation time. Some sight deficiencies also become worse at night.

Tinted glasses should never be worn at night, nor should so-called 'night driving' glasses. When it is dark the eye needs to receive as much light as possible through the windscreen glass.

Clean windows

A dirty or scratched windscreen will be very much more likely to provoke dazzle than one that is kept clean. Clean all the windows, inside and out, before driving at night, and also clean your spectacles if you wear them. When cleaning a windscreen at any time take care to avoid scratching it.

Auxiliary lights

Before considering the purchase of auxiliary lights it is worthwhile making sure that the existing lights are functioning as efficiently as possible. Check that the lenses are clean and that the reflectors are in good condition. A straightforward improvement in headlight performance can be achieved by replacement of the tungsten bulbs with quartz-halogen ones. These give a very much more powerful beam. Yellow bulbs give no improvement to the performance of the lights.

Any auxiliary lights must be fitted according to dimensions specified by law. A spotlight mounted on the near-side used to be considered the best way to improve illumination of the kerb, but many of the modern auxiliary driving lights have a wider beam.

White reversing lights are very useful accessories if your car is not fitted with them. These can be connected in such a way that they are switched on when you engage reverse gear.

Use of dipped headlights

Dipped headlights should be switched on as dusk approaches. No economies are made by delaying switching them on as it gets dark, and their use enables other road users to see you. Even if other traffic has not put on its lights, if you believe the visibility is such that it will be safer to use them, do not hesitate to do so.

Dipped headlights should be used unless the street lighting is of a high standard. They should certainly be used when there is no street lighting at all (where the streetlights are farther apart than 200 yards). The lighting, in some places, is uneven, leaving pools of darkness which could conceal a pedestrian or parked vehicle, and dipped headlights would pick these out. They should always be used on motorways at night, even if the motorway is illuminated.

When following another vehicle your lights should always be dipped (you should never turn the headlights off). You should also keep sufficient distance from it that you do not dazzle the driver through the reflections of your lights in his mirrors. (Your dipped beams should fall just short of the rear of the other vehicle). When overtaking, do not switch to main beam until you are at a point where you will not dazzle the driver of the overtaken vehicle. When you are overtaken, dip your lights as soon as the other vehicle is past.

You should always be the first one to dip your headlights when another vehicle is approaching you with his lights on main beam. If he does not dip his lights at all, on no account retaliate by attempting to dazzle him with your lights on main beam. A quick flash of your lights may remind him that he has forgotten to dip. It is courteous to dip your lights for cyclists also.

Dipping your lights for oncoming traffic should be carried out early on left hand bends, because your light beams meet the other driver's eyes before he is very far into the bend. Right hand bends, however, give you slightly more time on main beam before you run the risk of dazzling the other driver.

When it is possible you should quickly return to main beam in order to give yourself the best possible visibility. There is no point keeping on dipped beam when driving on unlit roads where there is little traffic.

Avoiding dazzle

Most people find that their eyes are drawn involuntarily to stare directly at the lights of oncoming vehicles. Firm determination is needed to stop yourself doing this and to force your eyes to look straight in front of you directed at the nearside kerb.

The risks of dazzle are reduced if you keep the windscreen scrupulously clean (as well as your glasses if you wear them for driving). Keeping the lenses of your lights clean and the lights correctly aimed will also minimise the chances of your seriously dazzling other motorists.

When driving on main beam you can prepare yourself for the reduction in visibility which happens when you dip your lights, by carefully studying and remembering as much of the road scene ahead as you can while your lights are still on main beam. Your speed should be such that you can stop within the distance you can see in your dipped beams to be clear. If you are dazzled, or cannot see far enough ahead, you should

Driver's view using dipped beam

slow down, even if you think you will hold up following traffic by doing so.

You may find yourself dazzled by vehicles coming close behind you or not dipping their lights. If you have a dipping mirror, switching it over will help to alleviate the irritation, but do not forget to switch it back again once that other vehicle has gone. When it is in its dipped position, it becomes very difficult to estimate the speed or distance of following traffic. If you do not have a dipping mirror, moving it slightly to one side will divert the reflection, but, again, you should re-align it correctly once the other vehicle has gone.

Driving at night

You should prepare yourself, as well as your car, for any journeys at night. Remember that your judgement of the speeds of other vehicles will be affected since you have only their lights to base your judgements on. It is frequently difficult to be sure about the precise position of some lights in the distance. Your estimates of your own speed will also be affected—it is not uncommon for your car to seem to be going faster at night.

Any long journey, particularly late at night, is likely to make you

Driver's view using main beam

fatigued. Eat only light meals beforehand, stop at regular intervals on the journey (at least every three hours) to take a refreshment break or some brisk exercise. Do not take any drugs or alcohol, and remember that your body's alertness falls to its lowest peak in the early hours of the morning. Keep the car well ventilated, and if you feel you are becoming drowsy, pull off the road (not onto the hard shoulder of a motorway), and either have some exercise or a short sleep.

Although it may appear to be easier to spot other vehicles at night, it is an unfortunate fact that a large proportion of the vehicles on the road have lighting defects. You should therefore be constantly on the alert for vehicles, including cycles, with no lights, or only one light, or very dim and dirty lights. You can easily make a dangerous mistake if you act on first impressions under these circumstances. You could also find unlit vehicles parked on dark, country roads. Flashing your lights on the approach to a crossroads is a useful warning signal to other drivers that you are there. It is no more than that, however.

Make sure there are no bright lights in your car to distract you when driving at night. In rain, the problems of dazzle will be worse because of the multiple reflections of all the other lights, and, in addition, stopping distances will be increased. Extra caution is called for in this case.

Consideration for other drivers can be exercised at night by thoughtful use of your indicators. If you are in a queue of traffic waiting to turn, unless you are the first or last in the queue, other drivers

will be grateful if you do not allow your indicator to continue to flash unnecessarily. Keeping your foot on the footbrake, in addition to being bad practice, will also have the effect of dazzling following drivers with your brake lights.

You should also be particularly watchful at night for pedestrians, children, animals and vehicles pulling away from the kerb.

Breakdown

In the event of a breakdown at night, get the car off the road if possible. The hazard warning lights should be switched on if the vehicle is likely to obstruct other traffic, and an emergency triangle should be set up 50 yards behind the car (150 yards on the hard shoulder of a motorway). It is always wise to carry a torch in the car for any unexpected incident at night.

Parking

You should not park on the road at all if there is somewhere else convenient to leave the car. Do not leave your vehicle on the right hand side of the road at night (except in a one-way street). Switch off your headlights when you stop to avoid the risk of dazzling other motorists.

Cars, motor cycles and other vehicles under 30 cwt unladen weight can park at night without lights provided that:
a the road is subject to a speed limit of 30 mph or less
b no part of the vehicle is within 15 yards of a road junction
c the vehicle is parked close to the kerb and parallel to it, and, except in a one-way street, with its nearside to the kerb.

Rain

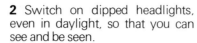

Wet weather driving demands gentle use of all the main controls —steering, clutch, brake and accelerator—and a larger-than-normal allowance for errors and emergencies. The presence of rain means reduced visibility, a deterioration in the car's stopping ability and increased risks of skidding and aquaplaning.

Rain is most dangerous when it falls after a long dry spell on to roads that have become polished and smooth. The water blends with oil and rubber deposits on the road surface to form a mixture on which the risks of skidding are greatly increased.

Remember that the soles of your shoes will be wet when it rains and that they will slip on the control pedals. Scuff them on the carpets or matting to give you a better and safer grip on the pedals.

Basic rules

There are four basic rules which apply to driving in the rain:

1 Reduce speed so that you can manoeuvre safely through bends, roundabouts, busy road junctions and in mixed traffic.

2 Switch on dipped headlights, even in daylight, so that you can see and be seen.

3 Use windscreen wipers and washer, and also if necessary, demisters and screen heaters to maintain the best possible forward and rearward vision.

4 Do not change speed or direction suddenly, or a slide may be induced.

Visibility

Visibility in rain is all-important. The wipers will often clear light rain from the windscreen with a few sweeps, but then if they continue on an almost dry screen they can leave smears of drying dirt. Use the windscreen washers liberally and operate the wipers in short, frequent bursts.

Heavy rain, on the other hand, can overload the wiper blades, allowing an almost continuous sheet of water to flow over the screen. Reduce speed even more than you would otherwise have done. If the reduction in visibility is severe, pull into a side-turning or lay-by until the storm passes. This usually takes no more than a few minutes.

Rain can also cause windows to mist up inside the car. The windscreen is easily cleared by the demister, by fresh air or by the use of an impregnated cloth. Above all, when visibility is reduced, switch on dipped headlights.

Adhesion

No one has yet perfected a tyre whose grip in the wet is as good as it is in the dry. Nevertheless, some good modern tyres have wet grip as good as the dry grip of some tyres made in the 1960s.

The grip of a tyre on a wet surface depends on two factors:

Tread: the grooves in the tread dispel most of the surface water. The greater the tread, the more water can be displaced, and yet as the car travels faster, larger amounts of water must be pumped through the grooves.

Sipes: These allow the tread to act as a squeegee, mopping up the quantities of water left by the tyre's main grooves.

The area of contact of a tyre on the road is very small, about the size of a large footprint. The space between the neighbouring groove flanks on a crossply tyre changes significantly as it rolls through its contact patch. The faster the speed, with these tyres, the more restricted the drainage passage becomes.

This change in tread pattern is negligible with radial ply tyres because all the deflection takes place in the side walls. This is why radial tyres tend to give a better wet grip than crossply ones. It is, nevertheless, not uncommon to have a difference in emergency braking stopping distances in the wet of up to 20% between radial tyres of similar tread patterns but made from different types of rubber. Thus, allowance should be made for the

Tyres	Stopping distance in feet	Type of road
Good tread pattern	190 feet	Dry smooth concrete
Good tread pattern	310 feet	Just wet concrete or polished asphalt
Tread depth 1 mm	460 feet	Just wet concrete or polished asphalt
Tyre grooves filled with oil/rubber sludge	760 feet	Just wet concrete or polished asphalt
Tread depth 2 mm	360 feet	1 mm water on road surface
Near bald	1,360 feet	1 mm water on road surface
Crossply tyre tread depth 4 mm	490 feet	2 mm water on road surface
Radial ply tyre Tread depth 4 mm	420 feet	2 mm water on road surface
Crossply tyre tread depth 4 mm	990 feet	4 mm water on road surface
Radial ply tyre tread depth 4 mm	570 feet	4 mm water on road surface

Scale (stopping distance in feet): 100, 200, 300, 400, 500, 600, 700, 800, 900, 1000, 1100, 1200, 1300. Thinking distance 60 feet.

fact that the braking performance of the car in front and that of the car behind may differ markedly from yours.

Trucks and coaches, particularly older ones, have braking characteristics which are inferior to those of cars. When they are lightly loaded they tend to swing out of line, so they should always be given a wide berth.

The tyre's grip depends on the weight on the tyre as well as on the adhesion between the rubber and the road surface. Abrupt changes of direction or speed have the effect of transferring weight from one tyre to another and this

can upset the handling and braking balance of the car in the wet. It could reach the point where the driver loses control.

The road surface is another important consideration for the driver in the wet. The uneven cracks in coarser surfaces tend to fill with concrete dust, rubber and oily deposits, particularly during a dry, hot summer. A downpour of rain can turn this into a thick sludge which clings to and fills the tread grooves.

The tyres perform in a most peculiar fashion under these conditions. The road adhesion is even lower than on a water-covered surface,

since the tyres cannot bite through the film on to a hard, continuous surface.

The only practical way to deal with this sludge is to wash it out with a strong jet of water over the tyres.

Reduce speed

There are several reasons for driving more slowly in rain:
1 The grip of the tyres on the road surface is reduced.
2 Directional stability is impaired, and a sudden slide is not uncommon when braking or accelerating rapidly.
3 Compared with a dry road it takes longer both in time and

distance to pull up on a wet surface, especially when you are travelling fast.
4 Rain can impair visibility, particularly through side and rear windows and the dirt-speckled areas of the windscreen not swept by the wipers.
5 Rain tends to muffle the sounds of other traffic, which are frequently the first warning to the driver that there are other road users not far away.
6 Pedestrians, in trying to escape from the rain, tend to dash across the road without taking due note of other traffic. In addition, they frequently overestimate the ability of motorists to brake safely and avoid them.

Rain

Periods of heavy rain can induce conditions for which many motorists may be unprepared. As far as possible, of course, one should try to avoid these situations, but there could be circumstances when it is valuable to know what to do should the unexpected take place.

Unfortunately the phenomenon of aquaplaning is not as rare as it should be. Much depends on the condition of the tyres as to whether or not it will occur. The importance of good tyres is nowhere more evident than in this situation.

Aquaplaning

How does aquaplaning occur? As the car is driven at speed into surface water, it builds up a cushion of water ahead of the rolling tyre. If the tread grooves cannot allow sufficient water to be passed through them, the tyre will lose road contact and float off on a wedge of water. The action is like water skiing, depending on forward speed.

Aquaplaning speeds

40mph
Smooth tyre, crossply or radial

45 mph
1mm tread depth crossply or radial

55–60 mph
7–8 mm tread depth, new crossply

65–75 mph
7–8 mm tread depth, older pattern radial

85–90 mph
Radial with drainage channels

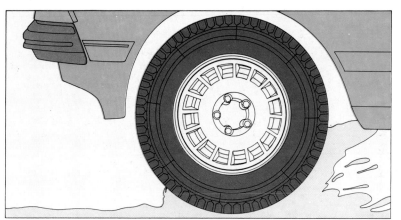

Once you are aquaplaning, the application of brakes or steering becomes ineffective, for there is no solid surface for the tyres to grip against. Ease off the throttle and brakes until the speed drops sufficiently for the tyres to make ground contact again.

The speed at which aquaplaning may occur depends on the depth of water on the road, and the tread depth of the tyre. The minimum tread allowed by law in Britain is 1mm. Tyres with only 2mm of tread may become unsafe at normal cruising speeds, often due to the deteriorating state of heavily-trafficked trunk roads. Tyres with 3mm of tread are much less prone to aquaplaning, although on some roads the depth of surface water might be greater than 5mm in tracks left by heavy trucks. These conditions may be found in the slow lanes of dual carriageways and motorways.

Conditions of aquaplaning will be reached at different speeds for different types of tyres. In a situation where there was $\frac{1}{8}$in (3mm) depth of water on the surface of the road, the chart shows the speeds where aquaplaning occurred.

Contrary to popular belief, lowering the tyre pressure, far from helping, merely brings on aquaplaning at a lower speed.

Flooded roads

Driving into flood water at speed is almost like hitting a wall. You may lose control, then come to a violent stop, risking injury to passengers. However, provided the speed is not too high it is perfectly feasible to ford fairly deep water without loss of control.

If the water is no deeper than the bottom of the cooling fan blades—on average 10–12 inches or roughly to the centre of the wheel hub cap—it is possible to drive through it. Engage a sufficiently low gear, 1st or 2nd (L or l in an automatic), so that the engine can propel the vehicle through the water without risk of stalling.

Use about half-throttle and keep it constant, neither easing it off nor depressing it suddenly as you feel the resistance of the water. Keep the speed slow or moderate to reduce the water splash swamping the electrics and/or the air intake. If it feels as though the engine is about to stall, slip the clutch to keep it going.

Should the engine stall some water may be sucked back through the exhaust system into the engine cylinders. This could result in permanent and costly damage to the piston, connecting rod or crankshaft, and it may not necessarily manifest itself until 100 miles or so later.

Changing gear almost invariably means a change in engine speed and manifold depression, with a similar risk of sucking back water through the exhaust pipe.

Good observation, particularly at night, should give warning of flooded roads. Places where the road is undulating, or where there is a dip under a railway bridge, should warn you that rain tends to collect there quickly. If the contours of the fences, trees, hedges and buildings at the side of the road appear to be unnaturally low, beware of flooding, and slow down at once.

Immediately after passing through deep water test the brakes. They may be saturated, and only driving very slowly and braking lightly at the same time will generate enough heat to dry them out. Be sure they are pulling evenly on all wheels before building up speed again.

River floods

Should you be confronted with a fast-flowing stream which has burst its banks, do not panic, but try to estimate the depth of water, direction and the speed of its flow. Consider your car to be a shallow draught boat, and position it so that, allowing for the deflection caused by the current on the wheels of the car, you can cut across the stream to reach the opposite bank.

Should the water reach the height of the sills and the driving wheels thrash uselessly in the water you will be getting close to floating. However much it may run counter to your instincts, open a door, preferably on the down-stream side. This will reduce the unwanted buoyancy and allow the tyres to grip solid ground again. Do not let the engine revs drop, and above all, do not switch off.

Escape from a sinking car

If you have been swept out into really deep water, it will be necessary to abandon the car. You may find it very difficult to open the doors against the rush of water. The inside of a saloon car will hold sufficient of an air bubble for you to breathe while you deliberately prepare to abandon the sinking vehicle. The car will not drop like a stone, it will sink relatively slowly, heavy end first. In these few seconds you should:

* Free yourself and your passengers from all restraints such as seat belts and child safety harnesses. Use as little energy as possible in order to conserve the air in your lungs.

* Keep the heads of all occupants above the level of the water as it rises inside the car.

* Release all door safety catches.
* Wind down the windows to allow water pressure to equalise inside the car and out.

* Push the doors wide open and step out.
* Form a human chain and swim or float to the surface.

This method should also be used for escape from soft-topped cars, rather than making an escape hole in the canopy. The stays and brackets are so close together they could easily impede the upward exit.

Wind

Although the problems of driving in wind may not appear to be great, studies of accident figures have indicated that on some sections of road which are prone to windy conditions, a large proportion of the accidents which took place there occurred on days when wind conditions were worse than average, many of these accidents happening on the exposed sections of the road. A wind blows on most days of the year, even though strong winds are experienced relatively infrequently, and the experience of driving in strong cross-winds is sufficiently unnerving to justify every driver taking the subject seriously.

Observation

It will not always be immediately obvious that a wind is blowing, particularly if you have been travelling for some time and the wind has sprung up during the course of your journey.

The movement of the trees is not a consistently reliable guide to the force of the wind. Some trees do not deviate very much even in high winds, while others appear to be permanently bent in the direction of the prevailing wind. Unusual movement of roadside trees, however, will warn of the possibility of strong winds.

Other warnings of the presence of high winds come from observation of flags or bunting on petrol station forecourts, the effects of wind on the telephone wires, and the behaviour of other vehicles. If you see the cars ahead of you suddenly veer to one side, it is quite likely that there will be gusts of wind at that point.

Observation of the terrain ahead

Strong winds across the Severn

Trees blown by a high wind

Further evidence of wind

can also warn of the likelihood of strong cross-winds. If you are emerging from a section of road protected by trees or woodland on to an area of barren heathland, you could expect to be subjected to sudden cross-winds. Stretches of open motorway can also be crossed by strong winds.

Country roads

The main hazards of high winds when driving in country areas are not so much the deviations to which the car may be subjected, but rather more the risk of finding branches, twigs and even whole trees blown down in the road. Drive more cautiously than usual on minor country roads because of these possible hazards.

Towns

Gusts of wind in built-up areas will be very haphazard, appearing to come from almost any direction. Alleyways and narrow streets between tall buildings can funnel the wind into strong gusts across the road. These gusts will tend to blow rubbish into the air, and can blow pedestrians and cyclists off course.

Wind speed

The speed of the wind is generally given in terms of a force number. This relates to the Beaufort scale of wind force.

Beaufort scale wind force number	Wind speed mph	Description
0	less than 1	calm
1	1–3	light air
2	4–7	light breeze
3	8–12	gentle breeze
4	13–18	moderate breeze
5	19–24	fresh breeze
6	25–31	strong breeze
7	32–38	moderate gale
8	39–46	fresh gale
9	47–54	strong gale
10	55–63	whole gale
11	64–75	storm
12	75 +	hurricane

Motorways

The problems of driving in high cross-winds appear to be worst on motorways. The path of the road cutting across large areas of open country makes them more susceptible than other roads to cross-winds. Deflection of the wind by the parapets of the bridges can produce gusts appearing to come from all directions and requiring quick responses from drivers. The response should not be too violent, however, or the car could be provoked into a skid. You should, generally, reduce your speed in high winds.

Passing high-sided vehicles in strong winds is an unnerving experience. As you approach a high-sided vehicle you are steering a course which compensates for the strength of the side-wind. When you get alongside it, how-ever, and are shielded by the other vehicle, this force disappears, and you appear to be sucked towards it. In fact, this is because you were not steering a completely straight course, but were compensating for the side-wind. As you approach the front of the other vehicle the force of the side-wind will be felt again. This force is usually experienced at a point slightly behind the front of the other vehicle.

The most important thing to do when driving in such windy conditions is to avoid over-correcting the steering. Your tyres are very well able to handle quite strong sideways forces and you retain control better by working with them rather than against them. The main danger to avoid is allowing the path of your car to be blown sideways such that it gets in the way of other traffic.

Roof racks

The use of a roof rack will always affect a car's handling, particularly in windy weather. In addition it will also increase fuel consumption even when the rack is empty. All luggage placed on a roof rack should be well fastened as low as possible to optimise air flow over the car. Make sure the roof rack is securely attached to the car.

Caravan towing

Towing a caravan can be particularly difficult in high winds. If your speed is too high and your caravan is not well-loaded a cross-wind can induce the phenomenon of 'snaking'. The appropriate course of action to take is described on pages 186–187.

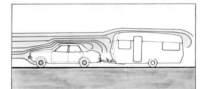

Experiments have been carried out with 'spoilers' fitted to the roof of the towing car to see whether this will improve the airflow over the caravan and therefore reduce its drag, improve its stability and reduce overall fuel consumption.

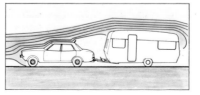

It has been found during tests with models in a water tunnel that a shaped spoiler, fitted at an angle of 45° as far back on the roof as possible (or 30° if placed farther forward) will direct the airflow over the caravan.

Lights in fog

The most important reason for using lights in fog is not in order to see better, but so that you may be seen by others. For this to be effective, all lights need to be kept clean, in good working order, and accurately aimed.

Headlights

The use of dipped headlights when visibility is restricted is mandatory in Britain and many other countries. This is especially important in fog, as they allow your car to be seen by other road users before its shape is evident.

Sidelights should never be used on their own under these conditions. An area of fog reduces the amount of light which can penetrate it, and effectively blocks out such a low-powered light source, so rendering the car invisible.

The main, full beam of the head- lights should also not be used in fog. The angle and spread of the beam is such that the fog particles will reflect a large proportion of the light back into the driver's eyes, severely dazzling him. Modern headlights with their sharply cut-off dipped beam provide as effective a performance in fog as many fog lights did eight to ten year ago.

The quality of the light emitted by the headlight depends more on the cleanliness of the lens and the brightness of the reflector mirror than on the wattage of the bulb. Whenever the weather is bad, as in fog, all lenses should be cleaned at regular intervals to remove caked-on dirt.

It is especially important in fog to avoid dazzling other motorists. Modern headlights are of great optical precision, and must be carefully aimed for this reason.

Sidelights alone barely show up in fog

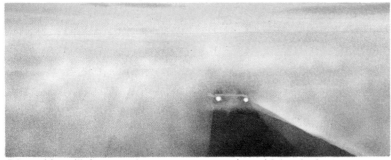

Dipped headlights are always necessary when driving in fog

Fog particles

The water vapour in the mist clings to minute particles of dust or dirt in the air to form fog particles. These then attract more moisture and, in turn, get bigger. These fog particles:

*float or drift with the slightest change in local air pressure or temperature

*absorb sound

*act as a series of half-mirrors

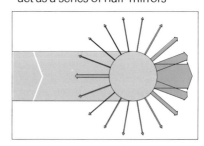

When a beam of light (pale blue here) hits a fog particle it is scattered in all directions. The thickness of the dark blue lines shows what proportion is scattered in that direction.

The last effect means that each particle reflects light hitting it from, for example, a headlamp beam. But it also allows some of the light to pass through it to the next particle, where the same thing happens. Some of the reflected light returns and hits the eye of the driver, and some of it is scattered in other directions. In addition, the light beam cannot penetrate far through the fog layer. The denser the fog the more the scatter and the less the penetration of the light beam. This is the reason why dipped headlights are more effective in fog than lights on main beam.

Fog lights

Visibility in fog can be greatly enhanced by the use of foglights. A pair of lights should be fitted, so that they indicate the width of the vehicle. If only one light is fitted, it must be used in conjunction with the headlights. This is to avoid the risk of possible confusion with a motorcycle.

Foglights should be mounted low on the front of the vehicle, in a zone which does not attract splash and road dirt. When they are not in use, protection against stones can be provided by a plastic cover.

The beam should be flat and wide with a sharp cut-off to prevent back scatter of the light. If a pair of lights is fitted, the nearside one should be angled on the kerb, about 15 feet in front of the car. The other one should be angled about two or three degrees to the right, so that it will pick up cat's eyes and lane markings.

Fog lights need to be cleaned regularly, when driving in fog. The spray from the vehicles in front, aerodynamic forces sucking up dirt, and the heat generated by the bulb all combine to form a thin coating over the lens which progressively reduces the amount of light passing through it. In some conditions, a 50% reduction in light intensity can take place within 30 minutes.

Rear fog lights

New cars now have high intensity rear fog lights fitted as standard. This regulation also applies to new caravans and trailers.

Not all other cars have these very useful lights fitted, and it is worth

Tail lights

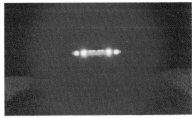
Rear fog lights

Rear fog lights with brake lights

Siting of rear fog light

considering their purchase as an accessory. In some cases, these lights have been wired into the brake light circuit, so that they come on simultaneously with the brake lights. This is dangerous.

The greatest danger in fog is being rammed from behind by a vehicle which was following too close. The intensity of a good rear fog light is such that it can be seen from about the same distance as that where opposing fog lights or dipped headlights would become apparent as a pair of small white specks. It is also about the same distance as that at which brake lights would become visible, and is about twice that at which a normal rear light or a clean reflector would be seen.

The intensity of the rear fog light should be about the same as that of a brake light, so that they will be seen together when the brakes are applied. If it is any brighter, the brake lights might not be seen in time. The lights should be fitted low enough not to dazzle following drivers. Their positioning is specified by law.

It is important that these lights should be switched off when it is not foggy and that they should be wired to a warning light inside the car clearly visible to the driver.

Law

Single fog or spot lights may only be used in conjunction with dipped headlights.

A pair of lights must be mounted equidistant from the centre line of the vehicle, and must be of the same colour, white or amber. The positions are defined as follows:

Vertically: At least 19·6 inches (500mm) from the ground. If the distance is less than this, they may only be used in conditions of fog or falling snow. The maximum height from the ground is 47·2 inches (1200mm). The lights must be permanently dipped, or capable of being dipped. They should not dazzle an observer 7·7 metres away with an eye level of 1·1 metres.

Horizontally: Cars registered before 31 December 1970: 13.8 inches (350mm) separation between the lights. Cars registered on or after 1 January 1971: 15.75 inches (400mm) maximum distance between the outer edge of the light and the edge of the vehicle.

Coloured lights

One of the less-commonly realised effects of fog is that it can change the colours which lights appear. Those at the red, amber and yellow part of the spectrum can pass through fog, although with some changes. Those at the blue and green end do not, however, and sometimes cannot be seen at all. So, in a dense fog, a red light may appear to be amber; an amber light might seem white; a white light almost green but a green light may not be seen at all.

Clean windows

In fog, as in all other adverse weather conditions, both the inside and outside of all windows should be kept clean and free of moisture. Use the wipers intermittently.

On the inside, you may usually rely on the car's ventilation system, but under really muggy conditions this may be too slow-acting or not powerful enough. It may well be possible to disperse the interior fogging of the windscreen by directing hot air on to it to evaporate the moisture. At times, however, it may be preferable to accelerate its condensation by directing cool air on to it and turning it into tiny water rivulets. Then warm air can be turned on to keep the windscreen unobscured.

Use a slightly damp chamois leather cloth to clean the windows, or a leather kid glove will do. Never use your hand, a handkerchief a tissue or a woollen or cotton glove.

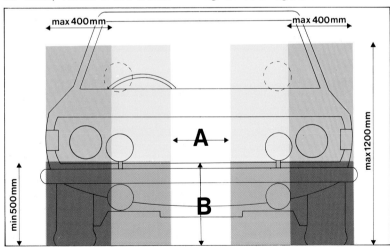

*Fog light positioning, Note **A** Cars registered before 31 December, 1970 may fix their lights not less than 350mm apart rather than 400 mm from the outside edge of the vehicle. Note **B** Lights sited less than 500 mm from the ground may only be used in fog or falling snow*

Fog driving

Fog provokes greater fear among motorists than most other adverse weather conditions, and with good reason. Not only does it strain all the driver's senses, but it also produces illusions to mislead him. Anyone who can avoid driving in fog is well advised to do so.

Why does fog form?

In Britain there is always some moisture in the air, and relative humidity rarely drops below 60%. A drop in temperature will cause the moisture in the air to form into finely-dispersed vapour droplets.

Generally, when the ground temperature drops fairly fast in relation to the air temperature, mists form and do not rise more than a few inches above the ground. Where the land has been warmed and there is little or no air movement, however, the mists may rise and hover over or drift across roads.

Air pollution from industrial plants, power stations or domestic heating appliances can turn this mist into a blanket of swirling fog. The fog blanket then acts as a heat shield, this prevents the cooling of the earth during the night from turning the fog into drizzle, and it also stops the sun's rays from warming up the ground sufficiently for the moisture to become re-absorbed in the air.

This situation can only be changed by strong winds or a substantial rise in the ground temperature. The moisture is then taken up in the air to form clouds.

Signs of fog

Fog tends to occur in early spring, autumn and winter when the heat of the sun is not sufficiently strong to vaporise the fog and lift it. But the situation can vary greatly along almost any route, so it is important to recognise the signs of fog formation.

Meadows, rivers, lakes, gravel pits and some woodlands can all give rise to fog. The moisture from freshly-tilled fields, however, can aggravate the situation still further. A substantial rise or fall in temperature and wind will disperse it. Early morning mists are soon soaked up by the summer sun, but less so in autumn and winter. If there is not sufficient change in heat during the day the fog can hang about for several days.

Fog driving rules

There are a number of basic considerations which should always be followed when driving in fog.

Lights: Immediately visibility becomes poor, switch on headlights, not sidelights. In fog, also switch on rear foglights, and front foglights (see pages 68–69), if fitted. Use dipped headlights, or you may be dazzled by the backscatter of the fog particles. Keep all lamp glasses cleaned regularly during a journey in fog.

Speed: Bring the speed right down. The correct speed for the circumstances will often be lower than intuition might indicate, and should always be the speed at which you can stop within your range of vision. This may be no more than 5 mph in some cases. Never drive faster than the safe speed, simply in order to keep in sight of another vehicle's lights.

Turning: Turning right is a particularly dangerous manoeuvre in fog. If it cannot be avoided, turn very carefully, signalling in good time. Keep a sharp watch out for

Dipped headlights and a slow speed are essential in fog

other traffic, and open the window to listen as well. Flash headlights or sound horn to be more certain your presence is realised.

Windows: It is important to be able to see as well as possible. Use the windscreen wipers, washers, demister, rear screen heater and rear screen wiper, if fitted. Open a window to prevent other windows misting up, and also for ventilation. The presence of fog will tend to make the car windows mist up on the inside. An open window will also help you hear other traffic.

Stopping: Take great care when stopping in fog, and always get off the road or carriageway. If you cannot avoid creating an obstruction, switch on hazard warning lights when stationary, and put out a warning triangle at least 100 yards behind the car (150 yards on a motorway or dual carriageway). However, do not hesitate to stop and park safely if the density of the fog is great. It will also be necessary to stop regularly in order to clean the windows and the lights, and this should also be done in a safe and careful manner.

Extreme care is required when turning or stopping

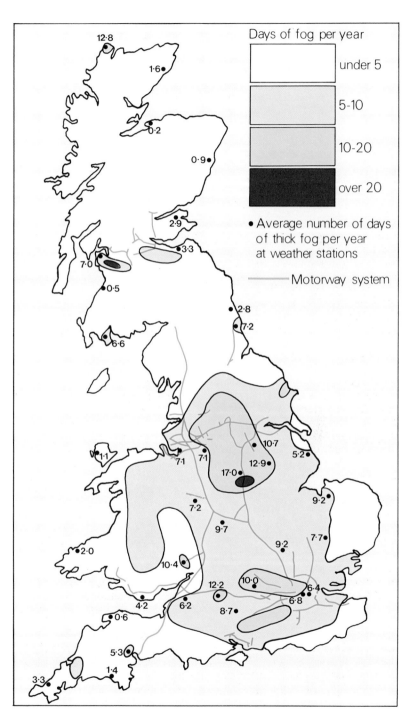

Days of fog per year

under 5

5-10

10-20

over 20

• Average number of days of thick fog per year at weather stations

—— Motorway system

Fog driving

Understanding how to drive safely in foggy conditions requires an appreciation of the psychological effects on the driver as well as due attention to safe driving. Knowing and recognising the illusions which fog can produce helps to combat their insidious effects, and these factors should be taken into account by every driver when travelling in fog.

Disorientation

Quite apart from the fact that fog makes it more difficult to see, there are other effects which are less obvious. These effects can all rob a driver of his sense of orientation.

Fog muffles sound; the denser the fog the more it absorbs sound. It is not until noise disappears that we realise how much we depend on it to warn us of the presence of other vehicles. It may thus be advisable to use the horn to warn any other vehicles which may

be unaware of your presence, particularly for example when making a right turn.

The other effects which fog has can add to the sense of disorientation. In the uncertain half-light produced by fog, trusted landmarks can become difficult or impossible to recognise.

In any case, it is always more fatiguing driving in fog. More concentration is called for, and the pulse rate, heart beat and sweat rate (an indication of stress) increase considerably. Many motorists drive faster and overtake more in order to get ahead of the queue, in the false hope that driving conditions will ease there. Usually, as weather conditions get worse, most drivers moderate their driving style, but this does not seem to occur in fog. This failure to reduce speed sufficiently undoubtedly contributes to the severity of accidents in fog.

Speed fallacies

Press reports of multiple collisions in fog tend to accuse the motorists of behaving irresponsibly, incompetently and dangerously. But why do motorists drive too fast in fog? Research has uncovered some possible explanations.

First, there is the theory of 'speed hypnosis'. When the fog blots out familiar landmarks and reference points a driver can lose all sensation of speed, and this is more pronounced on a featureless motorway than on a country lane with hedges on either side.

The subconscious fear of being run into from behind may cause the driver to speed up on the dangerous assumption that the situation is safe ahead. The result is that the speed becomes too fast for the prevailing conditions.

In thick fog, drivers have been shown to be unable to estimate their own speed correctly, or the distance between them and the

vehicle in front. For example, a driver believing he had reduced his speed from 70 mph to 20 mph was actually travelling at 48 mph.

To complicate this even further it has been found that fog produces the optical illusion of making objects appear to be farther away than they really are. Also, objects seen in peripheral vision appear smaller than they really are.

These different facts show how easy it is to misjudge not only one's own speed, but also the distance of other objects. The muffling effect of fog on engine noise distorts the information normally available from that quarter about the car's speed. It now becomes more than usually important to regularly refer to the car's speedometer (it is best for the passenger to tell the driver what the car's speed is). Add to this the optical illusion about the distances involved, and it can be seen how easy it is to drive too fast in fog. It can also be seen how to avoid doing so.

Not too close

Many drivers believe, erroneously, that the safest policy in fog is to keep within sight of the tail lights of the vehicle in front, and never to lose visual contact. This is often dangerous because it can result in the vehicles being too close together. When the front vehicle puts his brakes on, others may not be able to react quickly enough to avoid hitting the vehicle in front.

For example, suppose a line of ten vehicles were travelling at 50 mph in fog. The first driver sees a blank wall of white fog and applies his brakes. The driver behind him applies his brakes $\frac{1}{2}-\frac{3}{4}$ second later. This is repeated down the chain. The driver of the tenth vehicle will not apply his brakes until perhaps $7\frac{1}{2}$ seconds after the first driver. In that time he

will have travelled 550 ft farther than the first driver. Collisions are inevitable unless each vehicle in the chain was at least 55ft behind the one in front. Even if that were the case, however, not every driver may be alert enough to react within $\frac{3}{4}$ second, and some vehicles may have worse braking characteristics than others.

An additional hazard of following another vehicle in fog is that one does not get an accurate picture of the fog's density. The fog thins out immediately behind each vehicle, and it may suggest that visibility is sufficient to overtake this vehicle. When you pull alongside however, you may find you cannot see far enough ahead to complete the manoeuvre safely. This can lead to dangerous errors of judgement resulting in serious multiple accidents.

Fog at night

It is a mistake to drive on full beam during night time fog, not because it may dazzle oncoming traffic but because it may dazzle you. Dipped beam headlights should always be used.

In an urban environment with street lighting, the driver may be caught in a very difficult situation. The quality of the street lighting is important under some fog conditions—the amber light of the sodium vapour lamp is better than the blue-white light from the mercury vapour strip light. Depending on the quality of the street lighting, and the vertical thickness of the fog blanket, the motorist may find himself in a situation where there is a finely dispersed mantle of illumination everywhere, but no shadows. This makes it extremely difficult to pick out objects ahead or to the side.

Generally, the motorist relies on his headlights to pick out other objects, not only by illuminating them, but also from the shadows they cast. He can also observe the lights and reflectors of other traffic. In an urban situation when

it is foggy, these points of reference are missing, and orientation becomes much more difficult.

Freezing fog

This is the worst kind of fog. It usually starts as fog when the ambient air temperature is already quite low, about 2°C–4°C. As the earth cools, or in a cooling wind, the fog particles turn into frost, and are deposited on any surface as a thin covering of ice. A car driven through such fog soon tends to look like a box encrusted with icing sugar.

When the trunks and branches of trees begin to look white and glistening in the weak light, be prepared for that ill-defined mist ahead to turn into freezing fog.

In these conditions the windows tend to distort the already limited view. The windscreen washers may cease to work and the wipers often do not give a clear sweep either. Also, it is difficult to be picked out against a background of fog. The illuminating power of the headlights drops dramatically, and the roads tend to be covered in thin layers of black ice.

Fog appears deceptively thin in the wake of a large vehicle

Always conform to speed restrictions, especially in foggy conditions

73

Preparation for winter driving

Every motorist is likely to have to use his car during the winter months, so preparation for adverse weather conditions should be regarded as a matter of routine, rather than anything exceptional.

The first priority is to ensure that the car is in first class condition, and is well serviced. The driver should also prepare himself for driving in adverse weather conditions, by learning what he can, from books or courses, and practising the necessary driving techniques, off the road if possible. Much of the inconvenience brought about by severe weather can be minimised by careful forethought and by keeping a few simple items in the car.

Car preparation

A car that is well maintained and regularly serviced should have no problems with winter driving. Certain aspects of the car need special attention, however.

Air intake Some air cleaner inlets have summer and winter positions, and, if so, they should be adjusted for the winter.

Anti-freeze Although anti-freeze will last for two to three years, check before winter that the concentration is adequate for low temperatures. If the time has come to replace it, flush out the system thoroughly beforehand. Check all the hoses for possible leaks. Finally, do not forget to use a solution of anti-freeze and water when topping up the radiator during the winter.

Battery Cold weather reduces the performance of a battery. Clean the terminals and cover them with Vaseline, keep the electrolyte level properly topped up and re-charge it whenever necessary. When starting the car from cold, minimise the strain on the battery by applying the starter motor in bursts of no more than 5 seconds, followed by an interval of about 30 seconds. Turn off lights, heater blower, wipers and radio when trying to start the car, as these all take power from the battery.

Brakes Always keep the brakes in good order; any which work unevenly are especially dangerous on wet or icy roads.

Choke cable Extra use will probably be made of the choke during the winter, so make sure it works freely and that when pushed home, the choke mechanism is fully released.

Exhaust system Any leaks from the exhaust system could result in poisonous carbon monoxide fumes seeping into the car. The system should be checked at least every six months.

Fan belt The battery's problems in winter will not be helped if the fan belt is not correctly tensioned. Check its general condition and tension at the start of the winter, and always carry a spare.

Heater The heater will be subjected to extra use during the winter. See that the vents are not blocked with paper, dirt or rubbish, and also check that the hoses are not blocked or leaking.

Ignition system Damp in the winter months can affect the distributor cap, the low- and high-tension leads, the plug connection caps and the top of the ignition coil. These parts should be checked and thoroughly cleaned, before being given a protective spray of ignition sealing lacquer.

Lights The normal checking of lights should be more thorough than usual, and their aim should also be checked. Dirty road conditions will mean that they all need cleaning more often than usual. Keep enough cloths in the car for this purpose. Carrying a set of spare bulbs is especially important in winter.

Oil If a summer grade oil has been used, it should be replaced with winter-grade. A multi-grade oil will work just as well in winter as in summer.

Rear screen heater This useful item should be well cared for by cleaning it regularly with a damp cloth and a few drops of windscreen wash additive. If one is not fitted as standard, it is an accessory worth consideration.

Shock absorbers Worn or broken shock absorbers will seriously affect the car's handling and the tyres' grip, and will be particularly dangerous under slippery conditions. If the car bounces more than once when a corner is pressed down, the hydraulic damper is due for replacement.

Throttle linkages The smooth driving pattern essential for safe control and economical motoring cannot be maintained if the throttle is stiff. The linkages should be cleaned and lubricated, and any kinks in the accelerator cable straightened out.

Tyres Normal-use radial ply tyres will need about 3mm thread depth in order to cope satisfactorily with winter conditions. Apart from that, their general condition and pressures should be checked regularly.

Underbody Good protection of the underneath of a car will help protect it from the corrosion inevitable in a damp climate. Factory-applied PVC coating is the most effective currently available protection. The salt and grit used by Local Authorities in keeping roads free of ice and snow is a major factor causing bodywork and structural corrosion but dirt and dust particles are also important contributors.

Washers Windscreen washers get a great deal of use in the winter, and driving can be made difficult and dangerous if they fail. Clean the washer reservoir, the pipes and the jets, then fill with water containing a suitable additive which will help remove windscreen grease as well as prevent the water freezing. Check regularly that the reservoir is full. Do not use anti-freeze in the washer liquid.

Windows Clean windows are essential for safe driving, and they will need cleaning more often than usual in winter. It is also as well to check that there are no leaks which could let in water or exhaust fumes.

Wipers The blades should be cleaned and inspected for cracks. They may need to be replaced if they are more than 12 months old, or if they produce streaks across the windscreen.

Extra equipment

A survey of a wide range of accessories which help to make winter motoring safer and more enjoyable is given on pages 76–77.

There are many simple and inexpensive ways the motorist may reduce the inconvenience caused by winter conditions, which should be considered before winter sets in.

Anorak A useful precaution against getting wet or cold during an unexpected stop is to carry an anorak in the car.

Cloths A clean wash leather for the interiors of the windows and other cloths for the outsides and the lights will all be found necessary in winter.

Damp-start Starting difficulties can sometimes be overcome by spraying damp-start lacquer on to parts of the ignition system before starting the car.

De-icer Ice on the windows can be easily and quickly removed by the use of aerosol de-icer and a plastic scraper.

Driving shoes The heavier footwear appropriate for walking in snow or rain is not always ideal for driving. A pair of lightweight driving shoes should be kept in the car. It is also useful to keep a spare pair of waterproof boots in the car in case of emergency.

Jump-leads An extremely useful item to keep in the car is a set of jump-leads. Connect the positive terminal of your battery to the positive terminal of the other car's battery, and do the same with the negative terminals. Run the engine of one car and then turn the starter motor of the other. Take great care connecting and disconnecting these leads.

Lights Fitting extra lights to the front and rear of your car can make winter driving, especially in fog, easier and safer, although take care not to overload the battery. See pages 68–69 and 76–77. Keep spare bulbs in the car for all the lights.

Sacking Problems of getting stuck in the snow or on ice can often be overcome by driving over some sacking placed under the wheels.

Scraper A plastic scraper is an almost essential item for clearing the windows of ice and frost.

Shovel Digging away the snow down to the road surface may be the best way of getting going on a difficult surface, and folding-type spades are inexpensive.

Snow chains Under some circumstances of deep snow, a set of snow chains or snow-grips can be an asset.

Torch It is always useful to keep a torch (in working order) in the car, not merely during the winter.

Tow-rope It may be possible to help stranded motorists if a good, strong tow-rope is carried. It is unwise to use it for tow-starting another car, however.

Tyres A set of winter tyres may be helpful, even necessary, under extreme conditions. See pages 76–77.

Prepare yourself

Although some winter conditions require considerable care, adequate preparation can prevent them from becoming an ordeal. The preparation of the car, and planning for winter motoring, will remove many travel uncertainties.

The more a driver can study how to deal with wintry conditions, the better equipped he should be to deal with them. If frost is likely and the car is parked outside, leave the car in gear, chock the wheels and release the handbrake before it freezes in the on position.

It is wise to start to think about your journey further in advance than usual. Avoid routes which include steep hills and uncleared roads in snowy conditions. Minor roads with relatively little traffic, however, may not be too difficult to negotiate after snow, as it will not have been compacted into ruts. In foggy and swirling snow conditions, try to avoid right turns.

Winter driving accessories

It is usually possible to avert most of winter's difficulties by planning and thinking ahead. Neglect of one's car can often lead to problems, and a few simple precautions will usually remove the worry of being unable to complete a journey. A wide range of accessories is available to help ease the problems of winter driving and these are surveyed here.

Getting started

One of the more basic aspects of winter protection for a car is the addition of anti-freeze to the cooling system. A mixture of 25% of anti-freeze in the water will give sufficient protection for usual conditions of frost, but in extremely cold circumstances the ratio should be increased to a $33\frac{1}{3}$% solution.

Topping up should be done using water and anti-freeze mixed in the same proportions. It is best to leave anti-freeze in for about 2-3 years, and then flush the system and completely replace it with a fresh charge.

Window cleaning

It is always important to be able to see clearly out of the car, never more so than in winter.

An ice scraper is essential for removing frost from the windows, although frosting up can be minimised by covering the windows with newspaper before leaving the car in the evening. The scraper should always be cleaned after use to remove any grit that may have been collected.

An aerosol can of de-icing fluid will remove the need for laborious scraping, although if it is kept inside the car, frozen door locks may make it difficult to reach. A lock mechanism may be unfrozen by heating the key with a match or cigarette lighter.

Windscreen wiper blades wear out after about a year, if they are used frequently. Many replacement blades are available. The tension from the wiper arm spring reduces after a time, so the arms need to be

periodically changed. Wash-wipe kits are available to clear the rear window, and so are rear screen heaters, if one is not fitted as standard on the car.

The screen wash reservoir should always be kept topped up. Special additives will minimise smear and prevent the washers freezing.

A manual screen washer can be converted easily to one which is electrically-operated by means of a simple kit.

Tyres

The most important consideration when preparing for driving in winter is that all tyres should be in good condition, with adequate tread. This should, of course, be the case all through the year.

Winter-treaded tyres are a useful accessory for those who drive in rural areas, where snow, slush or mud can be expected for part of the year. Some of these can be used all year round, but they tend to be noisy on dry roads and wear out more quickly than standard profile tyres. It may be preferable to change to summer tyres once the severe weather has passed. Studded tyres are the ultimate for severe conditions, although their use is illegal in certain countries. They do, however, cause severe damage to the road surface if they come into contact with it.

Detachable chains and clamp-on snow driving aids are not widely used in Britain, but are compulsory for certain sections of mountain roads in Europe. Practise fitting them before driving in snow.

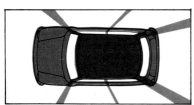
Vision with clear windows

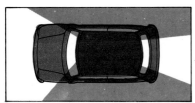
Restricted vision when only small areas are cleaned front and rear

Winter tyre tread may be pre-moulded for stud holes

Studs fixed in tyre

When studs are used only 1·5mm should protrude above the surface

Snow chains in use

The spring steel grip is quickly fitted for emergency use

Lights

Extreme weather conditions can seriously limit visibility. Before contemplating buying additional lights, however, you should check that your standard equipment is working properly. All the bulbs or sealed beam units should be functioning correctly, the reflective surfaces must be in good condition, and you should see that none of the lenses is cracked and letting in water.

Quartz-halogen bulb conversion units make a great improvement to ordinary headlights. These bulbs produce more light for the same wattage than conventional bulbs.

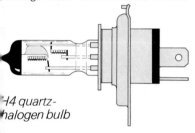

H4 quartz-halogen bulb

The greatest care should be taken when handling quartz-halogen bulbs. The touch of a finger on the quartz part of the bulb can seriously reduce its life, and, if accidentally handled, it should be cleaned with a rag soaked in methylated spirit before being fitted.

Fog gives rise to the most worrying visibility difficulties. Special fog lights, whose beam is very wide

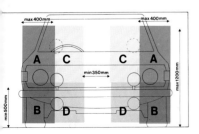

but cut off at the top to reduce back-scatter, are widely available. The light may be white or amber, according to choice.

A very sensible auxiliary light is the rear fog light. A pair of these should be fitted, and all new cars are required to have at least one. They should not be wired in such a way that they come on with the brake stop lights. More details about the fitting of fog lights are given on page 68.

Auxiliary driving lights are now more commonly used than spot lights. They give a wide spread as well as penetration up the road, in preference to the narrow, pencil beam of the spotlight.

Reversing lights are another very useful accessory. No more than two should be fitted, and they can only be used when reversing. The use of a fog or spotlight for this purpose is prohibited. The bulbs in these lights should be no more than 24 watts in strength.

Control of reversing lights is usually automatic from the gearbox. Where this is not the case, there must be a warning light on the dashboard or on the switch.

A wise precaution is to carry at least one spare bulb for each of the main lights. This will save a great deal of inconvenience in the event of bulb failure.

Cars registered after 31.12.70
Fit lights in area A. If in B use only in fog or falling snow.
Cars registered before 31.12.70
Fit lights in areas A or C. If in B or D use only in fog or falling snow.

The range of the dipped head-lights' beam

Switching to main beam improves vision at night

Auxiliary driving lights provide greatly improved vision

Snow and ice

Brief spells of snow and ice are not uncommon in Britain, nor are isolated areas where deep snow and drifting occur. Local Authorities generally keep the motorways and principal roads free of snow, spreading grit and salt to turn the snow into slush, or using snow ploughs to deal with deep drifts.

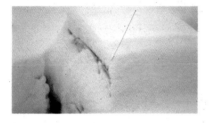

Starting off

1 Be sure to remove the snow and ice from all windows and mirrors. Clearing a small patch on front, rear and some side windows is not enough. The complete window surface needs to be clear, and wing mirrors should have the ice scraped off them.

2 If the car has been parked out-of-doors, direct hot air from the heater against the windscreen before heating up the car interior. Heat the rear window as well if possible.

3 When attempting to start the engine apply the starter for up to 5 seconds with a long pause in between, rather than using a series of short, sharp bursts. Then, pull away as soon as possible to help the engine, transmission and the car itself warm up quicker and avoid wasting fuel.

4 Do not drive in boots which have accumulated deposits of snow or ice. They are often quite wide, they will slip on the pedals and you will lose any sense of feeling. It is better to change into a dry pair of soft shoes for driving.

5 Select the highest gear possible when moving off, usually second. Let the clutch out gently to avoid wheel spin. If wheel spin occurs, ease off immediately. The tyre tread can only bite when the wheels revolve slowly, and in cold conditions, the rotating wheels may turn the snow into ice. The front wheels must be straight to offer the least resistance.

6 Be sure to use headlights if visibility is in any way reduced.

Driving on ice

One of the most frightening experiences while driving is to find suddenly and unexpectedly that you are driving on ice. It should not be sudden or unexpected, however, because good observation can warn you of your approach to an icy stretch of road.

The first thing to remember on a cold day is that although your car may feel warm inside, the temperature outside could be at freezing point or below. Watch for any indication that ice could be about, looking at puddles by the side of the road, and reading the

road ahead for areas which are more prone than others to the formation of ice patches.

The patches of road under over-hanging trees are unlikely to feel the warmth of the sun, and ice is likely to persist on the road there until well into the day. Where there is danger of falling rocks there can also be the possibility of ice on the road in winter, because rocks are often dislodged by water.

Your ears will also tell you when you are driving on ice. Unlike the swishing sound made by the tyres as they roll through water, on ice there will be much less noise and no swishing sound. In addition the steering will feel very light. To maintain control and stop the car skidding use all the controls very gently indeed. Make no sharp or sudden movements. Allow a great deal of extra space for braking by looking well ahead and anticipating the actions of other road users. If the car slides when you brake do not panic, but release the brakes immediately, even if it takes courage to do so. Then re-apply them quickly but extremely gently.

Steering and braking

It is important to know the nature of the snow-covered road surface you are driving on. Slushy snow has a high moisture content and a texture rather like a viscous fluid. It offers reasonable resistance to movement but little sideways control. As it is squashed down on to the road surface, tyres with insufficient width and depth of grooves will tend to fill. Road grip will be poor and intermittent, resulting in some loss of traction. This calls for gentle throttle, brake and steering application to prevent the car sliding out of control The granular type of snow neither compacts nor adheres to other

layers, and should be treated in the same way as sea sand. It is easy to sink into it when driving a car shod with ordinary tyres. Wide tyres spread the load, making sinking less likely.

Soft snow is relatively harmless—tyres can bite into it well, and it is not always necessary to drive slowly. A hard-packed snow surface demands much greater restraint, but most dangerous of all is a snow-covered road with ice underneath. Three inches of powdery snow on top of an icy road surface may prove more difficult than six inches of crunchy snow.

The important guide for both steering and braking in snow is to do both very gently, but never to do both at the same time. Either steer or brake. Braking distances may well be 3 times those experienced on dry roads, but on icy roads these braking distances can be increased by as much as 10 times.

All steering should be careful and slow. In order to get going, it is usually best to have the wheels as straight as possible. In a difficult situation, when it is necessary to steer and brake, avoid locking the wheels. First brake gently, then release the brakes; turn the steering wheel gently and then apply the brakes again when the vehicle is moving in the right direction.

When braking, apply feather-light pressure, and remember that the driver behind may not have such good brakes or tyres as yours. His vehicle may also be heavier and more difficult to control. Using a gentle pumping action minimises the risk of locking up the brakes and the flashing of your brake lights provides a more effective warning of your actions.

Do not be misled into believing that it is better to slow down by changing to a lower gear. The action of letting in the clutch can cause the vehicle to skid, as the engine braking is transmitted to the driving wheels which may be having a difficult enough time.

Traction

Modern car tyres are generally suitable for all-year-round motoring. Their ability to deal with powdery snow and ice is, however, limited.

A snowfall in Britain is frequently followed by gritting and salting

to keep most motorways and principal roads free of snow. The grit and salt turns the snow into slush and water by lowering the freezing point. The heat generated when tyres run over it assists the melting process. Any delay in starting gritting operations makes the job much more difficult. The surface layer turns into ice when the temperature drops and snow gets compacted by the traffic into ruts. Further de-icing salt and heat generated by the passing traffic is then required to melt it.

When the road temperature falls to around −5°C, the heat generated by the passing tyres fails to turn the snow into slush. Under these conditions, the half-melted snow fills the tyre grooves, and lowers their grip on the road. Increasing the pressures by around 20% sometimes helps in the case of

wide grooved radial tyres, but lowering them locks in the melted snow.

Special winter tread tyres are better at coping with roads covered with a layer of dry snow. A fairly open tread pattern allows the snow to be flung out in spurts. For very severe conditions a chunky pattern may be preferable. Heavily ribbed tyres are unsuitable for fast motoring on dry roads because they heat up quickly at speed.

Snow

For many people driving in snow is relatively rare and best avoided if possible. During a severe winter, however, most drivers are affected in one way or another and for some motorists snow is a common aspect of winter driving. Nevertheless, the skills of handling a car on snow can be acquired by everyone prepared to practise and these skills will always stand them in good stead.

Climbing and descending hills

An important attitude to winter motoring is to have confidence and consistency of driving style, particularly when tackling snow-covered hills. A steady speed should be maintained since to stop might cause trouble not only for yourself but for those behind. Avoid having to change gear half-way up the hill, so engage a low gear earlier than you would normally do. Removing the foot from the accelerator can have the effect of applying a brake.

If you do get stuck, going up a hill or on the flat, it is important not to persist in spinning the wheels. This can have the effect of turning the snow to ice and will make it more difficult to get going again.

*Make a track in the snow by moving the car forwards and backwards. Otherwise, shovel the snow away from all four wheels.

*Straighten up the front wheels.

*Put sand or gravel in front of the driving wheels. Alternatively put twigs or sacks there.

*Get your passengers to help by pushing. They should not stand in the path of the twigs or sacks, as these may be thrown out with quite a force. At times they may need to steady the vehicle sideways because when it is stuck in a rut or in deep snow it may follow a path tending to slew it sideways.

*Engage second gear and use just enough throttle to get out of the rut. Once on the move do not stop to retrieve the sacks or to pick up your passengers until you are on firmer ground.

If none of these measures gets you going again, the only course left is to roll back, with care and as much warning as possible, to a more level part where the run-up to the hill can be resumed. Remember, however, that steering precision may be lost under these circumstances. Accelerate gently in second gear and avoid slowing down or stopping until you are on easier terrain.

In spite of the problems which beset drivers climbing hills, it is actually much more dangerous descending steep hills in snowy weather. In these conditions, your speed should be so slow that you are completely in control of the vehicle and can stop at any time. In general, you should select a gear lower than that in which you would ascend the hill. Be more cautious in applying the brakes than you would be on the level to avoid the risk of skidding.

Should you find that the slope becomes even steeper, it is best to stop. Then select a lower gear and proceed once more. When descending a steep hill it is courteous to give way to vehicles coming up it, but never apply the brakes hard or suddenly.

In heavy traffic on undulating roads it is advisable to plan the approach to hills so that you will not get stuck half-way up. This may mean waiting at the bottom of a hill until it is possible to make the ascent without interruption.

Snow drifts

If your car is stranded in deep snow or in a blizzard, it is always best to stay with it. The most important things to do are to keep warm and to keep awake. A hot drink chocolate and sweets all help. In order to keep warm use everything that is to hand. Wrap yourself in blankets, carpets, sacks; even newspaper stuffed into your clothing will help to retain body heat. Be careful to avoid carbon monoxide poisoning when running the engine to heat the car interior. Only run the engine and the heater if the exhaust pipe can be kept clear of snow. Occasionally, open a window slightly (on the side which is free from drifting snow) to let fresh air into the car. Violent exercise or allowing yourself to drop off to sleep are both to be avoided. Conserve your energy and keep a channel of fresh air supply open if your vehicle is likely to be trapped and engulfed by increasing drifts.

If several other drivers are trapped in the same predicament, it is advisable for groups of people to sit together in one car, rather than in isolation.

Snow chains are quick and straightforward to fit

Snow traction clamps are intended for use in emergencies

Studs fitted to tyre

Close up of studs

Studded tyres

Special tyres fitted with hardened steel studs or spikes can be effective when driving on ice, but are of little practical use on deep, soft snow. Many countries limit their use to certain periods of the year, or ban them altogether, because of the damage they can do to the road surface.

If the studs come into contact with the road surface, they wear grooves which quickly fill with water when the snow melts, or during summer showers. These can cause the serious hazard of aquaplaning.

Snow chains

Roads in hilly or mountainous areas are frequently left uncleared by snow ploughs, particularly if the snow fall is widespread. Snow chains or special snow traction clamps can be useful in these circumstances. Not all cars are suitable for the fitment of chains. Before fitting them ensure there is enough clearance in the wheel arch to allow unrestricted up and down movement and full steering lock when chains are fitted. Practise fitting them at home before use. The action of snow chains is to transform the tyre into a primitive type of track-layer, with each link biting into the surface. Forward traction is good, but the sideways force which they can develop is very limited. This makes for poor steering and, occasionally, a sideways lurch. Vehicles fitted with snow chains should be driven at moderate speeds only, particularly on dry roads.

Test yourself

Are you confident you can drive safely in all weathers? Do you know the points to watch out for in different weather conditions? The preceding section of this book has surveyed the driving hazards associated with all different types of weather conditions. The quiz on this spread gives you a chance to test your own knowledge.

1 When approaching a long tunnel, after driving in bright sunlight, how can you ensure the best vision in the tunnel?

2 What type of sunglasses are most suitable for driving straight into low sun on a winter afternoon?

3 If you are dazzled when driving at night, will it help your vision to wear dark glasses?

4 Is it necessary to dip your headlights earlier on a left hand bend or on a right hand bend?

5 If there is light rain after a dry period, why should you be especially careful?

6 Under what circumstances does aquaplaning occur?

7 When driving through deep flood water should you use a high or a low gear?

8 What should you beware of when driving in high winds on exposed motorways?

9 Does the use of a roof rack affect petrol consumption?

10 Why should you not follow the rear lights of another vehicle when it is foggy?

11 Do yellow lights penetrate fog better than white ones?

12 Why should high intensity fog rear warning lights not be wired up so that they come on at the same time as the brake lights come on?

13 What should you be especially careful of when driving in thick fog on a motorway?

14 Which gear should you select when you are driving up snow-covered hills?

15 Should your car become stranded in blizzard conditions, is it better to stay with the car or to walk to safety?

16 How can you tell you are driving on black ice and not merely on a wet road?

Answers

1 You will probably have been wearing sunglasses while driving in bright sunlight. If they are of the photochromic type they will not lighten instantly when entering the tunnel.

For a second or more they will remain dark and you will be unable to see. Ordinary sunglasses will also remain dark, of course. Your eyes, unaided, will adapt much more quickly to the darkness of the tunnel, so, if you were wearing sunglasses you should remove them before entering the tunnel.

2 Photochromic sunglasses are unlikely to be suitable for this task. Their darkening depends on the intensity of the light which, in this case, may not be quite bright enough. This darkening is also affected by the temperature and if it is on the cold side in the interior of your car that also may reduce the darkening effect. It is preferable, in these circumstances, to wear normal sunglasses.

3 Dark glasses should not be worn when driving at night. In some countries it is illegal to wear them. The amount of light available to the driver at night is very limited, and to reduce this light by wearing dark glasses is most dangerous.

4 On a left hand bend you should dip early. An oncoming car will cross the beam of your lights before you cross his. On a right hand bend you will not risk dazzling the oncoming driver until slightly later. Meeting another driver on a straight stretch of road, however, you should always try to be the first one to dip his lights.

5 The rain water mixes with the oil and rubber deposits on the road to form an extremely slippery surface film which can also fill the treads of your tyres. Be extra cautious in such circumstances and allow plenty of room for braking.

6 When the depth of water on the road is greater than the tread on the tyre there is a risk of aquaplaning. As the car's speed rises, a wedge of water is formed just in front of the tyre and the tyre lifts so that it loses contact with the road surface. It begins to slide along the surface of the water and stops rotating. Control of the car can then be lost unless the speed is reduced so that the wheels stop aquaplaning. The speed at which aquaplaning occurs depends on several factors, including the depth of the water on the road, but a critical contribution is made by the tyre. The more tread there is on the tyre the less the chance of aquaplaning at any given speed.

7 The important points to ensure when driving through deep flood water are that the car keeps going and that no flood water enters the exhaust pipe or the engine. It is best to drive slowly in first gear, minimising the bow wave and keeping the revs up (slipping the clutch if necessary).

8 There are several possible hazards to consider when driving in a high wind on a motorway. Exposed stretches of the road will be liable to cross winds, and side gusts will also be felt when passing under bridges. Buffeting will be experienced when passing or being passed by high sided vehicles, and it is important not to be panicked into making excessive steering corrections when this happens.

9 Yes, dramatically so. Even an empty roof rack can increase fuel consumption by up to 5%. The loading of a roof rack is important too. Try to keep the load as low as possible and arrange it so that airflow over the top of the car will be smooth. Do this by placing the smaller items at the front.

10 There are several reasons why it can be dangerous in fog to follow another driver's rear lights. Your eyes can become hypnotised by the lights, stopping you from looking in other directions in order to orient yourself. You will also be given a false impression of speed and this may result in your driving too fast. The fog in the wake of another vehicle is thinned by the passage of that vehicle, so you could also be led to believe that the fog is thinner than it actually is. In addition to all this, the driver in front may be going too fast for safety. It is much better to rely on your own perceptions of the conditions and drive at a speed which will ensure you can stop within the distance you can see to be clear.

11 They do not, in fact—the penetration of fog by yellow lights is less good than by white lights. Yellow lights produce less "glare" however and this may give an impression of good fog penetration.

12 Because their value is that, when switched on, they enable the car to be seen from a greater distance when it is travelling in fog. This is not achieved if they do not come on until the brakes are applied. The bulbs have a similar intensity to brake light bulbs, so it is unlikely that they will show up a braking car from a greater distance. There is also a fire risk from the wiring overheating. The most important reason for not wiring up these lights with the brake lights, however, is that it is against the law.

13 The most essential consideration when you are driving in fog is not to drive too fast for the conditions. Your subjective assessment of speed is extremely unreliable in fog due to the illusions it creates. Other vehicles travelling too fast can lead you to believe the fog is thinner than it really is. Look at your speedometer from time to time (or get your passengers to do so) and check that you are not allowing your speed to increase.

14 You should use the highest gear suitable for the gradient. Too high a gear will probably result in the need for a gear change on the hill which could result in your getting stuck. Too low a gear could produce wheelspin because of the greater degree of power available at the wheels.

15 In general, if you are some way from safety and the weather is bad, it is better to stay in the car. You will be able to keep warm better and rescue services will probably find it easier to locate a car than someone walking through the snow. When waiting in the car, keep moving and do not allow yourself to go to sleep.

16 When driving on a wet road you will hear a swishing sound from the tyres. This sound will not be present when you are driving on black ice. You should be expecting black ice, in any case, by observing the temperature, the nature of the road and the roadside ahead.

Safe driving

Causes of accidents

Accidents are rarely accidental. They may be unforeseen or unexpected events but they rarely happen by chance. They are caused by specific factors or combinations of factors, not by fate. It is often possible to determine their causes, and therefore many accidents could be prevented.

There are three general groups of factors which contribute to accidents: the road user, the environment and the vehicle. Of these categories, road user factors are the most important; ⅔ of all injury accidents are due to driver error. Environmental conditions, which include the road layout as well as the weather, contribute to just over a quarter of accidents. The vehicle, its loading and condition of maintenance play a leading role in just under 10% of all road accidents.

The role of the road-user is discussed at length in other parts of this book. The other two factors are analysed in detail here.

Many road accidents involve pedestrians, especially children

The road environment

In about one quarter of the adverse environmental conditions which contribute to accidents, the driver's vision is restricted. This restriction may be caused by buildings, the line of the road, or as the result of parked cars, trees, road signs, lamp standards or bollards.

Pedestrian accidents make up a major part of the urban road toll. The most effective and most expensive solution is complete segregation of pedestrians and vehicles, but this can usually only be achieved in a new town.

Road signs and markings

The design of road signs and markings is laid down by the Government so that the motorist is presented with a consistent set of signs and markings at any given situation. These should provide clear information about potential hazards, but they sometimes fail to do so. Poor siting or inadequate signs and markings contribute to around 15% of the environmental factors in the causes of road accidents.

The sign itself may be misleading. For example, a direction sign at a junction may suggest, by the relative thickness of the lines, that the minor road approach to the junction is, in fact, the major road.

The direction sign may be complicated. To read and understand an unfamiliar sign at a complex multi-road junction may require the motorist's complete attention for several seconds. During this time he may overlook hazards such as pedestrians and parked cars, thus increasing the likelihood of an accident occurring.

Reduced visibility

The human eye can, generally, adapt successfully to most levels of light during the day. Where bright, direct sunlight is present, however, glare can occur. Sun, dazzle and glare comprise about 4% of the environmental factors in the causes of accidents. This factor seems to be more prevalent in accidents involving turning manoeuvres, and those in which the right of way is violated.

Visibility is also greatly reduced when driving at night. Indeed, about 1 in 3 of all accidents occur during the hours of darkness. The severity of these accidents tends to be greater than for daytime accidents: the proportion of fatalities is almost twice as high at night. This increased severity is not due solely to the lighting conditions. The incidence of drinking drivers and pedestrians on the road is also higher at night.

Inadequate street lighting is associated with about 3% of the environmental factors in the causes of accidents, but is thought to be a much more important factor in pedestrian accidents alone.

Although it may not be readily apparent the main road turns right at this junction

In the summer, especially, road signs can become obscured by overhanging leaves and branches

A detailed signpost with a number of destinations can take several seconds to read properly

In some conditions of bright sun visibility is greatly reduced

Weather conditions

The roads in Britain are damp or rain-soaked for about 20% to 40% of the times of principal traffic flow, although there are geographical and seasonal variations. Even so, over half the road accidents occur in conditions when the roads are dry and the weather is relatively good.

Wintry road conditions reduce the density of traffic; most accidents in winter are the results of losing control and skidding

accidents. The three commonest causes are deflation before impact, inadequate tread or tyre combination and incorrect inflation (usually under-inflation). An ageing, un-used spare has been found to be a cause of danger since the rubber tends to deteriorate. Change round all the tyres, including the spare, at regular intervals to avoid this potential danger.

Tyre deformation due to kerbing

Water on the road surface greatly lengthens stopping distances and increases the risk of skidding

Rain: About 17% of all injury accidents occur in rain and double that number take place on wet road surfaces where it is not raining.

Rain causes increases in the numbers of accidents in daylight and to a greater extent in darkness. The numbers of accidents are always increased both in summer and winter when visibility generally is impaired. In daylight, wet road surfaces without rain, however, cause greater increases in accidents during the summer, when water accumulating on a highly polished road surface increases the chances of a vehicle skidding and causing an accident.

Snow and ice: Approximately 3% of injury accidents in Britain occur on snow-covered or icy roads. About half the vehicles in such accidents are involved in a skid

prior to the impact, usually because of harsh use of the controls. Snow usually reduces traffic flow by about 15% overall, but even so the number of accidents on snowy days increases by about 25% compared with dry weather. The main reason for this increase is the icy road surface rather than the falling snow.

Fog: Traffic flows in foggy weather are generally reduced by up to 20%. Around 1% of all injury accidents occur under these conditions. On both urban and rural roads accidents in fog, although they take place more frequently, in fact cause no more serious injuries than accidents occurring in clear weather. Only 3% of all motorway casualties occur in fog, although some of these accidents involve multiple collisions and the injuries may be more severe.

Vehicle defects

Vehicle defects and design do not form a major part of the causes of accidents and sudden component failure is rare. More commonly, the standard of a particular component, although apparently adequate for normal driving, is not good enough to cope in an emergency situation. Overall, mechanical failure is a contributory factor in about 1% of accidents.

Steering defects: Free play in the steering system is likely to affect seriously the steering performance of the vehicle, and contributes to the causation of less than 1% of all accidents.

Tyre defects: Despite the excellent performance of the modern products, tyre factors are involved in the causation of about 3% of all

Inadequate brakes: Even though it has been estimated that about half the cars on the road have inefficient braking systems, inadequate brakes are causal factors in only about 3% of accidents. Typical causes of poor braking are worn linings, chafed or swollen hoses, leaky pipes and cylinders.

Vision restrictions: A driver's vision may be restricted by condensation on the windows, thick windscreen pillars, stickers, and luggage or large passengers obscuring rearward vision. Vision restrictions are involved in the causation of less than 1% of accidents.

Lighting defects: These usually prevent a vehicle being seen easily by other motorists, rather than posing a problem for the driver. They contribute to the causation of less than 1% of accidents.

Other factors: Doors, bonnets and boot lids may open when the car is in motion, but normally the vehicle can be stopped safely.

Driving decisions

The situation shown here can be resolved quite safely, but it contains many ingredients which are potentially hazardous. The correct reactions and decisions made by the driver at different stages are bordered in yellow, and the incorrect ones are bordered in green.

Situation

Looking

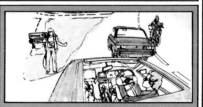

Seeing

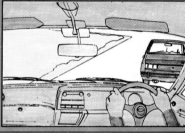

It has been estimated that drivers make about 10 to 20 decisions every mile, yet are rarely conscious of the fact. Driving should not be a matter of over-deliberate concentration all the time, however. This can provoke over-reaction. Driving decisions can be of an infinite variety, depending on the situation involved, but they all involve the same sequence of mental processes. Most accidents are due to driver error, so every attempt to understand why mistakes are made could help to reduce the number of accidents.

Every time a driver is faced with a changing situation or a hazard, four basic processes take place:
1 looking at the hazard
2 recognising the hazard
3 deciding how to cope with it
4 responding, using the appropriate controls.
A mistake in any of these four processes increases the chances of an accident. It does not necessarily mean that a collision will occur, because that depends on how the other traffic behaves, but nevertheless there is an increased risk of an accident.

Looking

Many different objects require or attract the driver's attention. Some, such as parked or moving vehicles, pedestrians and mandatory signs require action to be taken. Others, such as direction signposts, provide information, particularly for strangers. Many other objects are not directly relevant to the driving task, although drivers may, nonetheless, look at them.

The driver must not only look at the hazard, he must look at it in time to respond properly. In many accidents, by the time the driver has looked at the hazard, it is too late for any avoiding action to be taken. Under normal traffic conditions it takes only about $\frac{1}{2}$ second to 1 second extra anticipation time to be able to avoid 80% of collision accidents. This means looking farther ahead than many drivers tend to do.

Failure to look at the hazard is the commonest error committed by road users, and about one-third of all errors leading to accidents are of this kind.

The driver was usually looking elsewhere at the critical moment. Most people will look at things which are:
a important to them
b bright, colourful, or associated with a loud noise
c novel
d moving

All potential hazards should be important to a driver, but many of them, such as parked cars or pedestrians, are not novel and may be too easily taken for granted. Any distraction, however momentary, such as lighting a cigarette, turning to talk to a passenger, waving to a friend, looking at a

direction sign, or countless other examples, can lead to a collision if there is not enough space between the vehicles.

Seeing

We do not always see what we think we see. The brain must interpret what the eye sees, and if the image is indistinct or ambiguous, the brain may have difficulty in recognising it.

First impressions have a strong effect, particularly in traffic. A driver may continue to believe in his first impression of a situation until he is presented with

...ciding

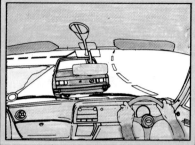

overwhelming evidence to the contrary. This error is known as 'misperception,' and it accounts for about 1 in 5 of all errors leading to accidents.

Many errors are misperceptions of the road environment. The general lie of the land, or inadequate sign-posting, may cause a driver to mistake the severity of a bend or the priority at a junction.

Misperceptions of the speeds or the separation distances between vehicles are common, particularly in conditions of poor visibility and when speeds are high. At night, or in rain, fog, slush or snow, dirty

Responding

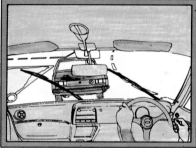

*Driver's errors: **looking**: does not see turning car; **seeing**: mis-understands intention of car, or does not see motorcycle; **de-ciding**: panic reaction or late braking; **responding**: operates the wrong control.*

rear lights producing a dim light may make a following driver believe that a vehicle in front is at a greater distance than it really is. In fog, vehicles tend to look smaller and further away than they are. The intensity of rear lights plays an important part in the judgement of distance.

A vehicle's position on the road is often used to predict its future movements. One close to the crown of the road may be assumed to be turning right, even if its indicators suggest otherwise. Illuminated brake lights are generally assumed to mean that the vehicle is stopping, rather than slowing to turn.

A common cause of motorcycle accidents is their not being seen by drivers turning on to a major road. Most car drivers expect to see cars on the road, and when they look to see if a main road is clear, they are looking for relatively large vehicles, not for small motorcycles often ridden close to the kerb. Many motor-cyclists now use their headlights and wear bright clothing to make themselves more conspicuous.

Accurate predictions of traffic movements about to take place are an important part of every driver's skill, but when rash as-sumptions are made without any confirming evidence, a potential accident situation is created.

Deciding

After the driver has seen a hazard and has recognised it correctly, he must decide on the appropriate course of action. Many mistakes can occur at this stage, but there are two general types.

One is the panic reaction. For example, when a hazard appears suddenly, the motorist, rather than reacting rationally, simply tries to stop as quickly as possible. He applies the brakes hard and often swerves as well, resulting in a loss of control of the vehicle. About 10% of errors are of this type.

A larger proportion of errors, about 25%, come about because of exces-sive speed with regard to the conditions. On approaching a hazard the driver does not reduce his speed sufficiently to negotiate it safely. Many mistakes of this kind are made on the approach to a bend or near the crest of a hill. The motorist may enter the bend too fast and then run out of road,

for there are limits to the sideways forces which tyres can exert to keep a vehicle on its chosen path.

Alternatively, the bend itself can cause a sight restriction, such that the motorist is unable to stop within his available sight distance. In most cases the radius of the bend, or the degree of sight restriction, is obvious a long way prior to the hazard, but usually, the reason why the driver was going too fast was an over-estimate of the road-holding capability of his vehicle, particularly on a damp or slippery surface.

There are many other errors made at the decision stage. They include delay in coming to a decision, incorrect overtaking, following too close, wrong evasive action, and changes of mind part-way through a manoeuvre.

Responding

The common error at this stage is to choose the wrong manoeuvre or, sometimes, select the wrong con-trol. A mistake such as pressing the accelerator when intending to press the brake is generally made only by novice drivers.

Confusion over the minor controls can result from the present lack of standardization. The positioning of dip switch, wiper, indicator and horn controls can vary from one car to another, and under stress conditions in a strange car, drivers may revert to old habits and operate the wrong control. In certain situations, such errors may be potentially dangerous for it takes 1 to 2 seconds to cancel the wrong action and substitute the correct one. About 1% of errors leading to accidents involve errors of response.

Reaction times

It is simple to explain what reaction time means, but it can be affected in so many different ways that it is easily misunderstood. It is the time taken for:

a the brain to receive information from the senses (eyes, ears and the sense of movement, as, for example, in detecting the onset of a skid);
b a decision on the course of action required (this may be a reflex action);
c transmission of the message to the appropriate muscles;
d response by those muscles.
The critical factor determining the reaction time is **b** the decision making process.

Reaction time varies greatly with age, experience, alertness and physical fitness. The same driver's reaction times may vary as follows:
0.6 seconds at the beginning of the day
0.8 seconds after a meal
1 second when tired
1.5 seconds after a few drinks or when taking drugs
2 seconds when drowsy or in poor health.

The standard reaction time is usually given as $\frac{2}{3}$ of a second. This translates into the thinking distance listed in the Highway Code, 30 feet at 30 mph, 40 feet at 40 mph and so on. This reaction time is not the same, however, for every driver, or for all circumstances.

Simple decisions

Where there is only one course of action possible, the decision is simple. After continuous practice, it may not be perceived as a decision at all. A driver at the peak of his mental and physical alertness can react in 0.3 seconds, if he is tensed to do so.

Choice situations

In most situations, there is a choice of reactions. The most likely response and the one the driver is prepared for will be the quickest. An unlikely response and one the driver is unprepared for will take longer. The reaction time will depend on the personal characteristics of the driver and the driving conditions, and reaction time can vary from about 0.5 seconds to over 2 seconds. Alternatively, the choice may be to do nothing.

Complex decisions

In complex circumstances the brain must fit together a number of different features of the situation before making a decision. Reaction times here are even longer than for situations where there is a straight choice of reactions.

Reactions in traffic

In heavy traffic the driver must be alert to many different eventualities. Normally, the stimulation of driving in traffic sharpens up one's reactions. Faced with a multitude of choices, however, the driver will respond more slowly than in a less complex situation.

No driver should depend on sharp reactions to keep him out of trouble. Sudden, emergency actions may catch other people by surprise, causing trouble for other nearby road users.

Excessive speed and very close following place a high premium on a driver's quick reactions. Events can happen so quickly that the brain and muscles simply do not have time to respond. The driver's attention becomes overconcentrated on too few events, and when something unexpected happens, such as a child dashing out from behind a parked car, the driver may be unprepared for this eventuality and react too late.

Following a line of vehicles for a long time can become monotonous which tends to slow reaction times. Drivers, attempting to keep their place in the queue, often follow too close behind the vehicle in front. It is easy for drivers to become so unalert that they fail to see the brake lights when the car in front slows down. This may result in a collision when rapid braking is required.

The good driver will anticipate traffic events and road conditions ahead so that he responds smoothly without panic. Good training and experience will produce fast reactions because the driver knows what to expect under different circumstances. This helps him to distribute his attention properly, to make the correct response when necessary. He will also be aware of what effect his actions will have on the safety margins of those around him, and thereby prevent others colliding with his vehicle.

Reaction time	Distance travelled at 30mph		Braking distance	Total	
0.6 seconds		26.48 feet	45 feet	71.48 feet	
0.8 seconds		35.30 feet	45 feet	80.30 feet	
1.0 seconds		44.13 feet	45 feet	89.13 feet	
1.5 seconds		66.20 feet	45 feet	111.20 feet	
2.0 seconds			88.26 feet	45 feet	133.26 feet

Overtaking

Some of the most difficult driving decisions are required when overtaking. Critical judgements must be made about the speed of the vehicle to be overtaken, the road conditions ahead, the distance and speed of any approaching vehicles and the acceleration capability of the vehicle being driven. The speed of other vehicles is judged by the rate of change of their perceived size.

As the situation becomes more complex and the decisions become more difficult, so the reaction time increases, possibly up to 2 seconds, for any situation with multiple options extends the mental sorting-out process. It would be lengthened still further by distraction, lack of driving experience, tiredness, alcohol, or the awkward siting of controls. As the delay is extended, so the chances of successfully carrying out the manoeuvre are reduced.

Age

Young drivers will usually have fast reactions, but lack of experience sometimes results in an unwise decision. If they make a mistake about a developing situation, they tend to persist in that error beyond the point where an older, more experienced driver would have introduced corrective action. In complex situations they may attempt first one course of action, then another. A delay of 2 to 3 seconds may elapse before the appropriate step is taken.

Reaction time is slowed down with advancing age. Experience can compensate to some extent, but both the under 25s and over 65s are at greater risk.

Eyes and ears

Good eyesight (particularly the ability to resolve fine detail a long way ahead, and good peripheral vision), and sound hearing, are essential for the brain to be able to perceive the road scene correctly and in good time.

Alcohol

The driver's reaction time can be affected in several ways by drugs and alcohol:

a it can blur his perception of moving objects and make stationary objects appear to be moving, lengthening his reaction time because the brain receives inadequate or inaccurate information

b it can produce badly co-ordinated responses, so that the physical actions take longer to perform correctly

c it can produce less caution, so the reaction may be the wrong one

d it can make the driver slow to respond to the unexpected

e large quantities of alcohol will cause tiredness, which slows down the reactions of both the brain and the muscles.

Fatigue

The responses of the brain and the muscles are both slowed down by fatigue. A less-commonly appreciated effect of fatigue is to make the driver give less attention to important events than they deserve.

A common danger for tired drivers is not seeing a bend, driving off the road at corners, or running into stationary objects.

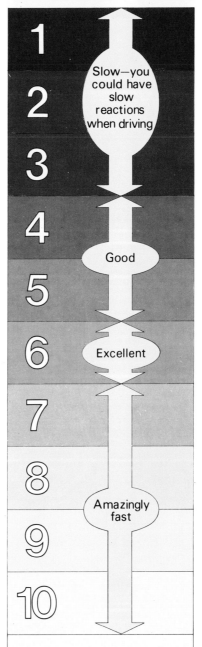

Test your own reaction time

A very simple test of visual reaction time is to make a ruler marked as shown. Ask a friend to hold it up, and, without warning, to let go of it. You must then catch it, and the point at which you catch it can be used to indicate your reaction time. The higher up you catch it the slower you are.

Daily changes

The body's level of activity varies through the day in a regular fashion. For most people its activity and speed of reaction are highest during the late afternoon or early evening. Its activity lowest around 2am to 4am, when the person is normally asleep, so driving should be avoided in the early hours of the morning, particularly on a long-distance journey.

A better test of the problems of choice which exist in driving situations is to use two rulers, marked in the same way. The friend holds up both rulers, but only releases one of them, and, again, you must catch it.

Fatigue

Most drivers will admit they have experienced feelings of drowsiness, yawning and general aches and pains while driving. These are all symptoms of fatigue.

At the same time, it is possible for a driver to be seriously affected by fatigue, yet be totally unaware of the fact. He may not feel tired and may only have started his journey half an hour ago. Yet this short time is amply long enough, in certain circumstances, for his driving performance to have been badly impaired by fatigue.

There are many factors which can bring about fatigue. Drugs or alcohol will make these effects worse than they might have been.

How to recognise fatigue

Sometimes the symptoms of fatigue will be obvious. These will include a feeling of drowsiness and perhaps a feeling of fullness after a meal.

The onset of fatigue may be less well-marked, however. Many drivers, particularly commuters who regularly travel the same route, may suddenly find themselves at a particular spot on this route, without knowing how they got there. This is a warning of fatigue. They must stop for a breather and to stretch their legs before continuing the journey.

Another experience may well be familiar to those who use motorways a great deal. The driver will suddenly come to, and find himself bearing down on an obstruction ahead. He has to take rapid avoiding action, and this is a warning that he is seriously fatigued and must stop for a rest.

A high proportion of accidents

Early morning low point — Mid-day peak — Afternoon low point — Evening pe[ak]

6 7 8 9 10 11 noon 1 2 3 4 5 6 7 8 9 10

involving only a single car, particularly on long, straight stretches, is attributed to the driver nodding off at the wheel.

The effects of fatigue on driving performance are very subtle and can be quite startling. As time passes and fatigue gets hold, the driver pays less attention to hazards just outside his field of view.

His responses become more automatic and less adjusted to the different situations he meets.

Mental fatigue

It is not always sustained physical effort which brings on fatigue. Stress, worry, irritation and mental tiredness can also be important factors in provoking mental fatigue.

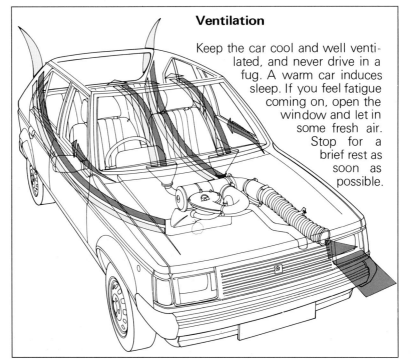

Ventilation

Keep the car cool and well ventilated, and never drive in a fug. A warm car induces sleep. If you feel fatigue coming on, open the window and let in some fresh air. Stop for a brief rest as soon as possible.

A violent argument before you set out on a journey, or, worse still, en route, will leave you mentally and physically limp and your driving performance will often deteriorate.

Even the weather can affect you— the atmospheric disturbance associated with heavy storms can make you irritable, susceptible to headaches and accident prone.

When below-par in your general health you are half-way to fatigue, even before you start driving. Any drugs you are taking, or the use of alcohol in these circumstances will hasten the onset of fatigue.

The mental stimulation involved in driving also plays an important part in provoking fatigue. Most people perform best at a middle level of stimulation. Low stimulation slows down all reactions, whereas a high degree of stimulation cannot be sustained for prolonged periods behind the wheel.

A monotonous period of driving may provide too little stimulation and could make the driver bored and drowsy. This is most likely to happen on an empty motorway, and particularly in fog, or at night when driving along the never-ending swathe cut by your own headlight beam.

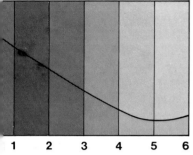

Early morning low point

1 2 3 4 5 6

Deliberately vary your speed, from time to time. Glance in your mirrors occasionally and listen to the radio set to a volume which does not obliterate the noise of other traffic.

Discomfort

Alertness begins with comfort and an uncomfortable seat leads to fatigue. Although the design of car seats is improving, it is, nevertheless, wise to spend a few minutes getting it exactly right to suit your individual requirements. Most drivers agree that in normal driving, your knees should be slightly bent, and the elbows also flexed with the hands resting naturally on the steering wheel. The correct driving position will provide a commanding, all-round view and leave you relaxed, yet alert. The head should be held straight to give the eyes an un-

obstructed, level gaze forward, and minimise strain to your back and neck muscles.

Both the thighs and the back need proper, firm support or physical fatigue will follow, bringing about discomfort or cramp. Adjusting the seat back, rake and runner position may help. Occasionally a back rest may do the trick, particularly on a well-worn car seat.

Long journeys

Use the Rule of Three:

Never drive for more than three hours without a break. Frequent short stops are better than one long stop. This interval between stops should be less if you are an inexperienced driver.

Do not aim to cover more than about 300 miles in one day, unless you are sharing the driving with another driver.

Beware of the third day away from home on a very long journey. At this time you will be at your lowest ebb, unwound from the tensions at home, but not yet refreshed. You may be irritable, and any arguments, particularly in the car, increase the risks of an accident. It is better to plan the third day as a rest-day.

Eat wisely

Too little food can be as risky as too much. Certainly, heavy meals before and during a journey should be avoided, as the digestive process leads to drowsiness.

Starting the day without a cooked breakfast, however, can be dangerous because of drowsiness resulting from the lowering of blood-sugar when the stomach is empty. This can happen whether you actually feel hungry or not.

Picnics en route provide a better way of eating. Even after a light meal, however, there is a little-recognised threat of tiredness. Some twenty minutes after the meal, a comfortable feeling of drowsy somnolence will be experienced. This could be dangerous when driving, so take a little physical exercise. Even a gentle walk will be sufficient before setting off again. Exercise tends to accelerate the circulation of the blood and speed up the digestive process.

Noise

Noise is always tiring. Rattles, body-drum and wind noise will quickly set your nerves on edge and induce irritation and fatigue. It is worth spending some time searching out the rattles, checking doors, window seals and panels for proper fit. Move any objects which rattle about or resonate, and alter your speed to get out of a resonance band.

Eye strain

If your eyes have to strain, peering through a dirty windscreen (or dirty spectacles), that strain will soon be transmitted to your neck,

body and limbs. Another cause of eye strain is insufficient illumination provided by the headlights. Equally, if you grip the steering wheel too hard, premature fatigue will be the result.

What to do

Understanding the causes of fatigue should help you to minimise the times when it will occur. Ensure adequate rest before starting a journey (avoid starting a long holiday journey after finishing work on Friday). Avoid driving in the early hours of the morning, when general body alertness is low.

Sit as comfortably and be as relaxed in the car as possible. Avoid heavy meals and stop every two or three hours.

If you feel tired, prepare to stop the car. Until you can do so safely, open the window, turn the radio on, talk to the passengers (or even yourself) in order to keep awake.

When your passengers notice the driver becoming strangely quiet, or see him driving erratically, they should realise he is tiring, and alert him.

Similarly, if you see another car behaving erratically, perhaps due to the tiredness of the driver, do not startle him with a sudden horn-blast or flashing of lights.

When you can stop, pull off the road into a lay-by. Do not stop by the edge of the road, or on the motorway hard shoulder. Go for a short walk to exercise the muscles and stimulate blood circulation.

If that does not help, have a sleep. Even a few minutes' sleep can have a reviving effect.

Driver's heart rate

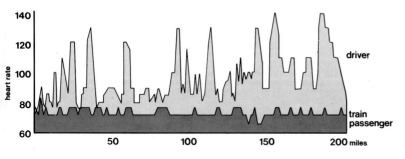

heart rate

140
120
100
80
60

50   100   150   200 miles

driver

train passenger

Illness and drugs

Any illness, however minor, will have a bad effect on driving ability. In some cases, even with a very minor ailment, such as a cold, the effect may be unexpectedly great, particularly if any medicine is being taken.

The driver's emotional state can also have an effect on his driving. A serious row before starting out can affect concentration, and bring on fatigue.

Driving licence requirements

Certain illnesses and disabilities preclude the issuing of a driving licence. These include the inability to read a number plate at 75 feet (if glasses are worn for this test they must subsequently be worn for driving), uncontrolled epilepsy (under certain conditions), liability to sudden attacks of disabling giddiness or fainting, any mental disorder requiring treatment as an inpatient, severe subnormality or mental deficiency. In addition, all drivers applying for a licence are required to declare if they are suffering from any other disease or disability likely to cause them to be a danger to the public.

Ailments and allergies: Coughs, colds, flu, hay-fever, asthma, other allergies, travel sickness, any painful conditions.

All will have some effect on driving performance, a lowering of concentration, an increase in reaction time, and possibly effects on vision. No one should drive with a high temperature or similar symptoms. Even a sneeze is a common, but little recognised driving danger. If it lasts for 5 seconds, a car at 70mph will have travelled 106 yards while the driver was almost blind and hardly in control. To stop a sneeze press a finger hard against the upper lip, or slap a thigh hard.

Car sickness is sometimes a problem for children, but the risks can be minimised by careful planning, avoiding rich food, keeping the children occupied, driving smoothly, and taking a break frequently (every hour). Ensuring correct tyre pressures, and soundness of shock absorbers and suspension will help prevent car sickness.

Emotional disturbance: Feeling 'one degree under', emotional problems, anxiety, tension, insomnia, depression.

It is not commonly realised that the subtle but common emotional upsets such as grief, anger, personal and business problems can seriously affect one's driving performance.

A wide variety of drugs is prescribed for anxiety and depression. The use of tranquillisers is widespread and increasing. These can have a marked effect on driving performance, by depressing the brain's activity, inducing drowsiness, fatigue and even mental confusion. Like all drugs, they should never be taken with even the smallest quantity of alcohol, if intending to drive. In certain conditions they may induce aggressive behaviour. Anti-depressants are being increasingly prescribed for mild cases of depression, but can make people take greater risks.

Women's problems: Pre-menstrual tension, period pains, effects of pregnancy.

The combination of irritability, depression and lethargy frequently found with pre-menstrual tension can have an affect on a woman's driving performance and could cause accidents. Everyone should appreciate that this is a time when reactions will be slower than normal and concentration will decrease. Tranquillisers may relieve the tension but should not be taken if driving.

Pregnant women should be able to drive perfectly satisfactorily provided they can adjust the seating position and seat belts to reach the controls comfortably and safely. In the later stages of pregnancy long spells of driving should be avoided.

Aches and pains: Toothache, stomach ache, migraine.

Severe pain, such as toothache, is usually thought to be insufficiently serious to stop one from driving. Yet, this pain together with the emotional struggle to 'keep going', can result in faulty judgement, loss of concentration and poor performance, all of them dangerous on the road. Many pain-killers, such as aspirin or distalgesic may affect driving performance.

Migraine is an even more serious problem. In addition to the pain, visual disturbances and nausea may be produced. Any sufferer from migraine should stop driving when he or she feels an attack coming on.

Drugs to avoid if driving: Amphetamines found in some nasal decongestants, inhalers, cold cures, tonics, appetite curbs, slimming pills; **Anti-histamines** found in some cold cures, asthma remedies, catarrh treatments, hay-fever remedies, travel sickness remedies, sea sickness pills; **Opiates** found in cough and stomach medicines.

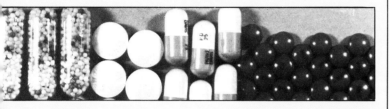

Drugs to avoid if driving: Sleeping pills some common brand names are Nembutal, Seconal, Sodium Amytal, Tuinal; **Tranquillisers** such as Equanil, Librium, Nobrium, Serenid D, Stelazine, Valium; **Anti-depressants** such as Marplan, Nardil, Noveril, Parnate.

Drugs to avoid if driving: Anti-histamines used in some preparations for the control of morning sickness during pregnancy; **Tranquillisers** such as Debendox, Librium, Nobrium, Tofranil.

Drugs to avoid if driving: Belladonna used in stomach medicines and indigestion mixtures and tablets, can seriously blur a driver's vision; **Anti-histamines** used in stomach medicines and travel sickness preparations; **Painkillers** such as distalgesic, aspirins and Aludrox.

Epilepsy

The sufferer from epilepsy may take out a driving licence provided he has been free from daylight attacks for at least three years, and that he would not be a source of danger to the public. Many epileptics take anti-convulsant drugs, and they should consult their doctor about possible side effects which may impair driving. Certainly, no alcohol should be taken with these drugs.

Nervous disorders

Nobody with a history of disabling giddiness or fainting should drive. Many nervous disorders develop progressively and patients should not decide for themselves, but should consult their doctor, in order to establish whether or not to drive. Those whose condition remains static for long periods may be allowed to drive.

Diabetes

Mild cases of diabetes, controlled by diet, should present no problems for the driver. All diabetics, whether the disease is controlled by diet or by drugs, should keep in their vehicles an adequate supply of sugar lumps, glucose tablets or semi-sweet biscuits, to avoid the dangers of a hypoglycaemic attack.

Heart disease

Anyone who has suffered a coronary thrombosis should not drive for at least two months after they have recovered. Angina sufferers, however, whose attacks are provoked by the exertions and frustrations of everyday motoring, should stop driving completely.

Hypertension should not affect driving ability apart from the side-effects of visual disturbances. Anti-hypertensive drugs, however, can impair driving, and a doctor's advice should be sought.

Orthopaedic problems

Stiff or painful joints, temporary or permanent, such as a stiff neck, can be hazardous while driving if they restrict the driver's normal movements. Backache can be highly distracting, but if its cause is by a bad seating position, a cushion or backrest may alleviate the situation.

Driving after medical treatment

A patient should never drive immediately after treatment which involves an anaesthetic, even in a minor case. A common effect on coming round is automatism, in which the patient appears normal, but is completely unaware of his surroundings.

For certain eye examinations, the doctor uses eyedrops to enlarge the pupil. These give blurred vision and the patient should not drive for several hours afterwards.

Drugs—Ask your doctor

So many different preparations are available, either over the counter or on prescription, that the only safe guide to their use while driving is your own doctor.

Alcohol and drugs

Alcohol should never be mixed with other drugs if driving. Tranquillisers and barbiturates are particularly seriously affected. Every patient should ask his doctor about the likely effects of mixing their drug with alcohol.

Vision

A driver receives most of his information about the road situation through his eyes. Certain minimum vision requirements are laid down before a driver may obtain a licence, but everyone should always remember that their eyesight may slowly get slightly worse as time goes on. Any suspicion of eyesight problems should be followed up without delay because of the serious implications for driving safety.

Legal requirements

In order to obtain a driving licence a motorist must be able to read a number plate from a fixed distance outdoors in bright daylight. The distance is 75 feet for number plate characters of $3\frac{1}{2}$ inches height (as commonly found on motor cars) and 67 feet for number plate characters of $3\frac{1}{8}$ inches height. This eyesight check is normally made at the beginning of the normal driving test.

If glasses are worn for this eyesight test they must be worn all the time when driving. The motorist is legally obliged to ensure that his vision remains up to the standard of this eyesight test.

Vision defects

The British number plate test is one of the most basic to be found anywhere, and is not very exacting. It demands only about one-third normal vision in one eye, in order to pass it.

Few accidents, about 1–5% of the total, are due to vision defects, even in part. Where they are involved, the situation is usually one in which the hazard is difficult to see, because of poor visibility or lighting, for example.

The major aspect of eyesight which is important for driving is the sharpness of the vision. This is checked with a distance test involving reading letters on a chart.

Long sight or short sight produce blurred images, and both these conditions are rectified by the appropriate spectacles, convex (positive) lenses for long sight and concave (negative) lenses for short sight.

Tunnel vision is caused by some eye defects. The normal visual field is about 160° but it can be narrowed to 90° or less in those affected by tunnel vision.

The most serious condition is the inherited defect of retinitis pigmentosa, which gradually restricts the field of vision until almost nothing remains. Sometimes, those affected compensate by moving their head from side to side.

Those afflicted with tunnel vision are not always aware of the fact. If only one eye is affected the other compensates. As peripheral vision is reduced, those with tunnel vision do not see objects such as pedestrians or vehicles outside the narrow field of vision, and this is a potentially dangerous situation. They will also find great difficulty when driving round corners. A similar effect to tunnel vision can be produced by wearing spectacles with broad sides. These are totally unsuitable for motoring.

Associated with tunnel vision is the phenomenon of night blindness. The periphery of the eye is used in night vision, and as this becomes affected in those with tunnel vision, night vision gets very poor indeed.

Colour blindness can have serious implications for motorists, particularly if it is not recognised. Men are more likely to suffer from it than women, and the most common defect is red-green blindness. Many people, however, do not realise they are affected. In many cases, colour blind people can drive satisfactorily, however, provided they are aware of the defect. Traffic signals can usually be interpreted by the position of the lights, and the movement of other traffic usually allows accurate interpretations of other lights.

Colour blindness is usually inherited, but it may be acquired by excessive pipe smoking, especially if coupled with high alcohol intake.

Good vision is absolutely essential for driving. The eyes are the most important of the driver's senses, as he receives 80% of all his information through them.

Many people think their eyesight is better than it actually is. It may have been good once, but it has probably deteriorated over the years. Surveys of large numbers of motorists have found that over 30% failed some aspect of an eyesight test and were advised to have a detailed eye examination.

No one need allow this situation to arise. A free sight test once a year is available to everyone under the National Health Service.

Those with only one eye should not drive until they have had time to adjust to using the single eye. Plenty of time should be allowed after any eye operation. Once the adaptation has been achieved, however, it is normally safe to drive, provided there is a full field of vision in the remaining eye.

Elderly people will probably suffer a deterioration in vision. This may not be recognised or admitted, and, if spectacles are worn, they may have become useless. All elderly drivers should have their vision checked regularly.

Distance test

The usual test for distance is to view a series of letters of carefully calculated sizes. The largest letter represents 1/10 normal vision, and inability to see it results in registration as blind. Can you read the centre row from 10 feet away?

75
A C E H
6
T L C N O
4
O D E C L

Visual field test

A simple test sometimes used by doctors is to face the patient, about 30 inches away; both doctor and patient cover their left eyes, and watch each other with the right. The doctor moves his forefinger steadily in from the right periphery, and then from higher and lower directions. The patient reports when he first sees the finger, and the doctor compares this with his own finding.

Normal sight The scene is sharp in the foreground and in the distance, with good peripheral vision and colour.

Short sighted The whole scene is blurred and out of focus, except for very close objects. Concave (negative) lenses are needed.

One-eyed vision The loss of one eye restricts vision on that side and affects distance judgement because stereoscopic vision is impossible.

Long sighted Distant objects are in focus but the foreground is blurred. The eye can correct this, but it causes strain and headaches. Convex (positive) lenses are needed.

Colour blindness The dangers of colour blindness are greatest when the defect is unrecognised. Several warning lights on the road may be missed by colour blind drivers.

Night blindness Those affected by tunnel vision are severely handicapped at night by a further reduction in night vision.

Tunnel vision This less common defect causes loss of peripheral vision and is potentially very dangerous. The view straight ahead is satisfactory, however.

Colour test

The simplest reliable colour test is the Ishihara Colour Plates, designed by a Japanese surgeon. The plates are filled with different coloured spots, some of which, in a contrasting colour, form the shape of a number. Colour blind people have difficulty distinguishing the number from its surroundings, or may be totally unable to recognise the number.

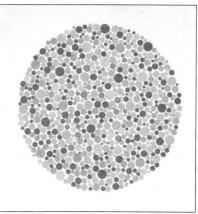

The safe car

Every year throughout the world, approximately 300,000 people die because they have come into sudden, violent contact with some part of the motor car.

During the last 10 years, increasing attention has been paid to the design of cars which limit the injuries inflicted on the occupants. Most modern cars give good protection for their occupants against front and rear impacts, and greatly improved protection against side impacts will be introduced over the next 10 years.

Pedestrian protection

As the protection of car occupants improves, so a larger proportion of casualties in accidents will be pedestrians, and riders of two-wheeled vehicles. Research is under way to redesign the car exterior to minimise injuries to this group of road users.

The height and resilience of the bumper is being studied, so that injuries to children as well as adults are minimised. The shape of the car combined with the car's speed affect the severity with which the pedestrian's head hits the car.

Steering assembly

The steering column and steering wheel can be a major source of injury to drivers in an accident.

The steering wheel might break, and the rigid steering column then act as a spear, transmitting the force of a striking object directly to the driver's chest.

Steering wheels are now designed to deform and distribute the blow over a contact area wide enough to avoid concentrated loads on only part of the chest.

A method of limiting the penetration of the steering column into the passenger compartment is one where the column has a number of flexible joints, which will readily break away in a collision. Alternatively, one element will slide down and over another when the front of the car is struck a severe blow.

In another very effective design the steering wheel boss is connected to the column through a fine mesh or concertina-type tube. When the driver's chest strikes the steering wheel rim, these collapse into a much shorter length tube.

Windscreen

The most common type of windscreen is made of toughened glass. This is cheap to produce, but in a crash it fractures into lots of small, round-edged pieces. These can cause serious injury, especially to the eyes, and the occupant is not retained by the glass, but travels through it. Forward vision is lost except for a pre-stressed, zone-toughened area in front of the driver.

Laminated glass, the other type commonly used for windscreens, is made from a layer of transparent plastic, sandwiched between two thin layers of glass. On impact it will not shatter across the screen but only produce a localised dent, resulting in no real loss of vision.

The car occupants are generally restrained by the windscreen and suffer less-serious lacerations than with toughened glass.

Whichever type of glass is fitted, if the windscreen gets dirty or smeared it becomes a safety hazard. Thin films of fine dust, dirt, traffic haze and tobacco tar on the windscreen all add to the problem of glare.

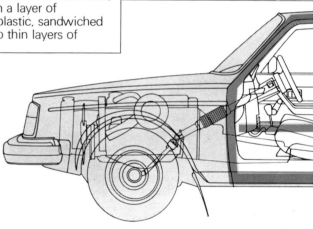

Mirrors

The interior rear-view mirror leaves substantial blind spots, depending on the size of the rear window. A mirror mounted on the driver's door is mandatory on new cars under UK and European regulations.

There is little point in fitting wing mirrors in addition to door mirrors. Wing mirrors can restrict forward vision, and endanger others. If used, they should be so positioned that the driver views them through that part of the windscreen which is swept by the wipers.

Slightly convex mirrors allow the driver to take in a wider field of vision, but convex exterior mirrors, combined with a flat internal mirror, can make judging size and distances difficult. The convex mirror makes objects appear smaller.

Head restraints

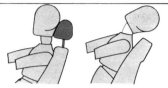

An effective restraint should be stronger than a mere head rest, and set high enough to be effective. In a head-on collision, a properly padded head restraint prevents the rear seat passengers from striking their heads on the front seat passengers or the seat frame.

In the much rarer cases of rear-end shunts, the passengers' necks are pressed backwards over the seat backs. This sudden neck stretching can cause a 'whiplash' injury to the neck vertebrae and the spinal cord. If the head is twisted back through more than about 90° it can be fatal. This injury can be prevented by a well-designed head restraint.

Blind spots

All-round 360° vision, even with the aid of external mirrors, cannot be achieved on modern cars. Attempts to reduce roof and door pillars and rear quarter panels to the minimum width possible, however, conflict with the requirements of overall rigidity, strength and occupant protection, to which these pillars contribute. International and national regulations lay down minimum requirements of driver vision and vehicle structural strength.

Fire prevention

Fire causes less than 2% of occupant fatalities, and the greatest danger is that of fuel spillage. An electric spark or a hot spot can set off the vapour. In many modern cars, the fuel tank is located inside the crush-resistant zone.

Should the interior trim of the car catch fire, there is a danger of asphyxiation due to the gases given off. Flame-retarding materials are now being included in car interiors.

Door locks

During a crash, the risk of injury to those thrown out of the car is five times as high as for those remaining inside. Many countries now demand that new cars must be fitted with anti-burst door locks. These restrain the doors from flying open, even in severe crashes, yet can be opened with ease by rescuers, in spite of the fact that the car may be severely mangled.

Another valuable safety feature for rear doors is the fitting of child-proof door locks. These isolate the interior door handle so that the door can only be opened from the outside.

The car structure

Cars are not made rigid all over, but are designed to have a strong passenger compartment with crushable front, side and rear zones. In an impact, the energy taken up in deforming these crushable zones reduces the forces transmitted to the passenger compartment, and hence the occupants. The human frame can withstand steady pressures much better than a sudden sharp blow.

In a collision between a small car and a bigger one, or a commercial vehicle, the occupants of the small car come off worst. Much research is being done to optimise the structures of cars of different sizes to give the best compatability for impacts of different kinds.

Seat belts

The wearing of seat belts by front seat occupants is compulsory in most European countries. It has led to a considerable reduction in both the number and severity of accident injuries, and also the saving of many lives.

What a seat belt does

When a moving vehicle suddenly stops, everything inside it, including the driver and passengers, will continue to travel forwards, unless they are restrained. The car occupants will be lifted more completely out of their seats, and will hit the windscreen or parts of the car interior.

The seat belt is designed to limit the movement of the car occupants as quickly as possible. The webbing stretches in a controlled way to help absorb some of the body's kinetic energy, and the loads generated are distributed over those parts of the body which can best absorb them with the minimum injury.

Wearing a seat belt

Some injuries are caused to drivers and passengers who wear seat belts, but have not adjusted them properly. Any excessive slackness allows the body to move some distance before the belt grips and thus can lead to bruises, abrasions and injuries of the soft organs of the abdomen, and allow contacts with the car interior which may produce injuries.

The lap section of the belt should always be comfortably tight and low across the top of the thighs, on or below the hard, bony area in the front part of the pelvis. Any load will be transmitted into this bony structure, which is quite capable of withstanding considerable shock loads. There should be no twists in the belt and the loads should not be transmitted directly to the abdomen, which cannot withstand them without injury.

The diagonal belt should also be comfortably tight with just enough room for one hand to be slid beneath it. The belt should run over the centre of the collar bone, not across the neck or upper arm.

The buckle should not be over the abdomen, but at the side of the hip, close to the pelvis.

The seat belt must be adjusted tightly because, in the few milliseconds of a crash, the body could easily move forward and hit something in the confined space inside a car.

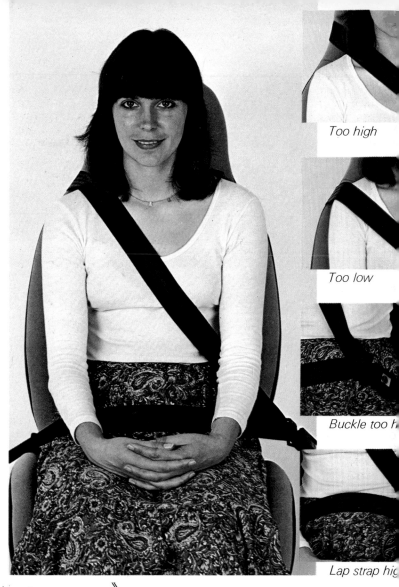

Too high

Too low

Buckle too h

Lap strap hig

Care of seat belts

A seat belt will not last for ever. It needs to be kept clean using warm soapy water, not petrol or white spirit. The anchorage points need to be checked regularly to make sure they are still secure and free from rust.

After a crash, the webbing will have been stretched. New seat belts should be fitted by a specialist and the anchorage points should be checked.

Inertia reel belts

Any inconvenience in wearing a seat belt is minimised by an inertia reel belt. These belts give a considerable degree of free movement, but they lock the wearer in a safe position when the vehicle stops suddenly.

The important factor in the performance of an inertia reel belt is its sensitivity. An oversensitive belt, which locks on too easily, can be a nuisance to the wearer. On the other hand, a system which locks only under severe emergency braking (upwards of 0·6g), allows too much webbing to be paid out before locking so that the wearer could hit some part of the car interior.

There are three types of inertia reel belts. Some are activated by the forces on the vehicle as it decelerates, some by the forwards or sideways movement of the wearer, and some combine the features of both types.

European regulations on the sensitivity of inertia reel belts allow easy disengagement while the car is stationary on a steep slope. They require a reel to lock at 0·45g.

Seat belt development

The effectiveness of seat belts could be further increased by eliminating the slack in the belt, and controlling the forces applied to the wearer with a load limiting device. At the moment of impact, the belt slackness is tightened up, usually by the firing of a renewable explosive cartridge. As the occupant moves into the belt, it yields by a small, but controlled amount by allowing a progressive tearing of a series of folded-over stretch joints. The shock load applied to the wearer is thus minimised. Should the cartridge fail, the restraint system works as an ordinary lap and shoulder seat belt.

Passive restraint systems

In an effort to overcome the reluctance of many people to wear seat belts voluntarily, several manufacturers are experimenting with various systems which work automatically, without the direct participation of the car occupants.

Airbags: these work by being explosively inflated when a sensor is triggered. After inflation, the occupant is cushioned by riding down on the bag which deflates under his load. Unfortunately, airbags are expensive to install and their reliability in service is still uncertain. The complex triggering system needs to be checked regularly for effectiveness, and this is expensive. The fact that airbags are not very effective in side-impacts, mean that a lap seat belt should always be worn.

Automatic belts: linking the belt to the car door as well as to the other internal anchorage points produces a system which automatically places a seat belt on the car occupant when the door closes.

Injuries without seat belts

Most serious collisions involve impact to the front of the car. Impacts from other directions are also important, but it is difficult to provide the same degree of occupant protection for side impacts.

The best protection is to minimise the side penetration and prevent the doors from bursting open as a result of the collision.

The passenger in the front seat runs the highest risk of injury if no seat belt is worn, the driver is next and rear seat passengers run the lowest risk. All these risks are reduced when seat belts are worn, and belts are now available for passengers in the rear seats as well as those in the front. The head and chest are most often damaged when car occupants who were not wearing seat belts are injured. Head and chest injuries are the most frequent cause of death in vehicle collisions.

It is sometimes suggested that being thrown clear of the car during an accident is preferable to remaining strapped in the seat. In fact, death or serious injury is at least twice as likely if the occupant is thrown out. Being trapped in the car if it catches fire is also most unlikely. Very few accidents involve fire, and all belt buckles are quick-release.

Seat belts should be worn on all journeys and at all speeds. The risk of accidents is actually greatest in built-up areas. Many injuries occur at relatively slow speeds.

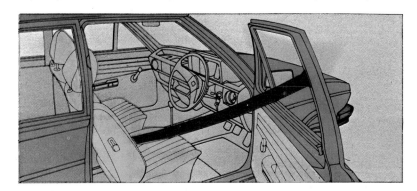

Safety accessories

Although thoughts of danger and accidents while driving are unpleasant, the prudent motorist can, nevertheless, acquire several accessories which will significantly increase his own and also his passengers' safety.

Seat belts

Front seat belts have been fitted to all cars since 1 January 1965, so almost every car on the road today should have them. Most cars have belts fitted with spring loaded inertia reels. These allow the wearer freedom of movement, but will lock during any sudden deceleration.

Spare parts for belts are not available, except through approved reconditioning centres, because seat belt manufacture is subject to very stringent BSI quality controls, to ensure proper functioning in an emergency.

Any belt which was worn during a severe accident should be immediately replaced. The stitching may have been strained, and the webbing over-stretched. A single belt can be replaced by an authorised fitting centre. Any new seat belt must bear the BSI 'Kite Mark' label indelibly.

APPROVED TO BRITISH STANDARD
BS. 3254

Rear seat belts

Mounting points for rear seat belts are frequently incorporated in current cars. Their advantage is that they protect the rear-seat passengers from being flung into the front seat or its passenger, during a frontal impact; they also protect the driver and front seat passenger.

It is possible to buy rear seat belts, and one very ingenious type of belt adjusts so that it caters for both adults and older children.

Child safety

In 1977, 9,741 children in Britain were killed or injured as passengers in cars. It is likely that only 10% of children aged 1 to 5 used any safety seat or restraint system.

The safest way for children to travel is properly restrained in one of the systems which has BSI approval, in the rear of the car.

A variety of systems is available. A small baby, up to sitting age (20lbs.), should be strapped into its carrycot, which in turn should be secured in the back seat by a webbing harness.

Children between 9 months (20lbs.) and approximately 4½ years (40lbs.) should sit in a child safety seat. Several different makes are available, although surveys have found big differences between their safety performance. A useful guide to the effectiveness of these safety seats is the BSI 'Kite Mark' label.

It is extremely important that the fitting instructions of these seats should be strictly followed. Parents who have fitted these seats themselves are advised to have them checked by a garage. An insecurely anchored seat would undoubtedly wrench free on impact, and the child could be injured.

Children aged between about 4 years (40lbs.) and 12 years (80lbs.), should wear a full child safety harness. These are suitable for all children too small to wear an adult belt and they have

Carrycot restraint

Child safety seat

Adjustable rear seat belt can cater for both adults and children

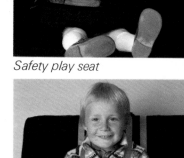
Safety play seat

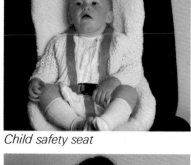
Child safety harness

shoulder and lap straps. Wearing these belts not only restrains the child safely but also encourages the habit of wearing a seat belt.

Breakdown warnings

Many new cars have, as part of their standard equipment, a hazard flasher system for emergency warning. A conversion kit is available for those cars not so

Emergency warning triangle in use

equipped, allowing all four indicator bulbs to be operated together.

Many countries require motorists, by law, to carry an advance warning triangle, although this is not the case in Britain. A robust red, reflective triangle on a strong base should stay up even in very windy conditions.

It can be stored easily in the boot, and, when needed, should be erected at least 50 yards (150 yards on the hard shoulder on motorways) away from the car on the lane it is partially blocking. Different European countries have their own regulations.

First aid kit

Many European countries require motorists to carry a first aid kit in the car. This is not the law in Britain, but it is a very sensible idea to carry one. The instructions should be studied when the kit is bought, then kept with it. The kit should be stored inside the car, preferably in the glove-box, rather than in the boot.

Fight fire

Nearly 20,000 cars a year go up in flames. Nearly one-third of these cases are due to faulty wiring, and almost as many to underbonnet petrol fires. Other causes are crashes or collisions, welding work, careless smoking and vandalism. It is a sensible idea to carry a fire extinguisher in the car, but it is important to ensure that it is effective. An aerosol extinguisher should be at least $1\frac{1}{2}$ lbs content.

Many aerosol extinguishers are filled with BCF liquid gas. This is bromo-chloro-difluoromethane, and is most effective. It is slightly toxic,

so if it is used in a confined space the area should be well-ventilated after the fire is out. It can be used also on electrical equipment. It evaporates completely, leaving no deposit, so there is no mess to clear up afterwards. BCF is generally better at putting out petrol fires than dry powder, an alternative extinguisher filling.

Every extinguisher should show its nett weight, so that the contents can be checked to ensure there is enough extinguisher material left.

The extinguisher should be mounted where it is accessible, such as in the driver's foot-well, or close to hand on the transmission panel. These positions are preferable to keeping it in the boot or under the bonnet.

Make sure you know how the extinguisher works before being

confronted with a fire. The contents of the extinguisher should be directed at the base of the fire, rather than generally over the flames. Starve the area of oxygen — open the bonnet just enough to be able to direct the spray at the base of the fire.

See better

The driver must be able to see properly all round the car. The windows must always be kept

clear. The inside of the front windscreen and side windows can usually be de-misted using the car's heater system. Wiping the glass with a damp cloth and a few drops of windscreen wash additive will usually clear off dirt and nicotine particles.

The rear windscreen can be cleared by using the rear window heater. If this is not fitted as standard, a range of different types are available as accessories, but they must be fitted with care.

The external surfaces of the front and rear screens should always be kept as clean as possible. The windscreen wiper blades should be regularly renewed, and the windscreen washer reservoir kept full. Anti-smear preparations can be added to the wash in order to improve its performance. Kits are also available for fitting washer and wiper equipment to the rear windscreen of some cars. Great care should be taken, however, to ensure that they are properly installed and electrically insulated.

Mirrors

Full all-round vision can only be obtained with the help of external and internal mirrors. A mirror fitted to the driver's door has become standard equipment on new cars. It has the advantage that it can be adjusted from the driver's seat, and it does not interfere with forward vision in the same way as wing-mounted mirrors.

In some circumstances, such as when towing a boat or a caravan, wing mirrors may be preferable. These should be of the boomerang type, springing back on impact. Where the trailer is wide, special mirrors are available.

Typical door mirror

Door mirror meeting EEC standard

Electrically adjustable door mirror

The internal mirror should be as good as possible. If the standard mirror fitted to the car does not give a sufficiently wide rear view, it should be replaced with one that does. Some mirrors can be found which give a very wide panoramic rear view.

A very useful type of rear view mirror is the dipping variety, which can be dipped at night to reduce the glare from the headlights.

Advanced driving

Many people who take a serious interest in driving wish to improve their standard of performance. The basic knowledge required by the driving test is only a starting point. The experience gained by having to deal with varied and complex situations helps to improve the standard, but there is only so much you can usefully learn on your own. For further improvement, expert tuition is the best method.

What is advanced driving?

A number of misapprehensions about advanced driving need to be dispelled. It does not involve very high speed driving nor does it consist of esoteric techniques such as may be used, for example, by a rally or racing driver. It requires developing a sympathy for the car and using careful planning and thought in order to drive safely and make good progress while keeping within the law.

It is sometimes believed that advanced driving techniques mean an increase in fuel consumption, but the reverse is usually the case. Even though achieving higher average speeds between A and B than an ordinary driver, an advanced driver will probably achieve better fuel economy through good planning and driving techniques.

Institute of Advanced Motorists

The aim of the Institute of Advanced Motorists is "skill with responsibility", and it is devoted to the promotion of road safety. All motorists are encouraged to take a pride in their driving. The key to membership lies in passing the advanced driving test and keeping up standards afterwards.

The Institute was founded in 1956 and is a non-profit-earning organisation, registered as a charity. It is run by a Council, the members of which are elected because of their expertise in various spheres of motoring. Their experience ranges from accident prevention, medicine, motor sport, the motor industry and trade, the driving schools, the motoring press, motoring organisations, the legal profession and Parliament.

Advanced driving test

The test lasts for one and a half hours and is conducted by one of the Institute's examiners. Some 95 test routes are located all over Britain and you can select the route most convenient to your home. You have to use your own car for the test. The examiners are all ex-police drivers holding Class I police driving certificates, and of all the motorists taking the test some 60% pass and join the Institute. As many women as men pass the test.

The test route measures about thirty-five to forty miles and incorporates road conditions of all kinds, including main roads, country lanes, urban areas and a short section of motorway where possible. The examiner will want you to drive in a steady, brisk manner, observing speed limits and driving with due regard to road, traffic and weather conditions.

Exaggeratedly slow speeds are not required, nor is excessive signalling. You will be expected to cruise at the legal limit when circumstances permit. Tests of manoeuvring skill such as reversing round a corner, are included and so is a hill start.

Observation forms an important part of the test and there will be one or two spot checks on this aspect during the test. There are no attempts to catch you out, however. You are free to give a running commentary if you wish to demonstrate your ability to read the road, but this is not a test requirement.

At the end of the test the examiner will give you an expert and candid view of your skill and responsibility, telling you whether or not you have reached the required standard. You will not fail for minor faults.

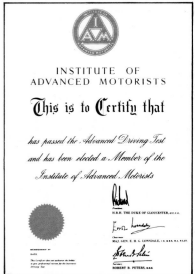

INSTITUTE OF
ADVANCED MOTORISTS

This is to Certify that

has passed the Advanced Driving Test
and has been elected a Member of the
Institute of Advanced Motorists

H.R.H. THE DUKE OF GLOUCESTER, etc. v.o.

MAJ. GEN. E. H. G. LONSDALE, c.b. m.b.e, m.a, f.c.i.t

ROBERT B. PETERS, m.b.e.

Technique	Assessment	Failure rate	Reasons for failure
Acceleration	Is your acceleration smooth and progressive? Is it excessive or insufficient?	12%	Uneven acceleration. Poor acceleration sense.
Approach	Do you approach traffic signals and other hazards correctly?	48%	Too fast approach. Coasted to compulsory stops.
Braking	Is your braking smooth and progressive? Is it late and fierce?	60%	Late brake application. Harsh handbrake application. Applied brake and changed gear simultaneously.
Car sympathy	Do you treat the car with care or overstress it?	40%	Not expressed in use of clutch, brakes and gears.
Clutch control	Do you co-ordinate your engine and road speeds properly? Do you ride or slip the clutch? Do you coast with the clutch disengaged?	48%	Ride clutch. Clutch slip. Coasting.
Gear changing	Do you change gear without jerking? If you have automatic transmission do you make full use of it?	38%	Harsh selection. Changed down with relaxed accelerator.
Gears, use of	Do you select and use your gears properly? Are you always in the correct gear before reaching a hazard?	72%	Late selection. Intermediate gears not used to advantage.
Hazard procedure and cornering	Do you cope with road and traffic hazards correctly? Do you turn corners properly?	78%	Incorrect assessment. Poor safety margin. Unsystematic procedure.
Horn	Do you use your horn and headlamp flasher according to the recommendations laid out in The Highway Code?	14%	Failed to use when required.
Manoeuvring	Can you reverse smoothly and competently?	28%	Lacked judgement and control.
Observation	Do you read the road ahead and drive accordingly?	58%	Late planning and assessment of traffic conditions.
Obstruction	Are you careful not to obstruct other vehicles—by driving too slowly, taking up the wrong position on the road or failing to anticipate and read correctly the traffic situation ahead?	8%	Loitering at minor hazards. Cutting in.
Overtaking	Do you carry this out safely and decisively, maintaining the correct distance from the other vehicles involved and using your mirror, indicators and gears properly?	38%	Too close prior to overtaking. Overtaking on bends. Overtaking in the face of other traffic. Cutting in after overtaking.
Positioning	Do you keep to the correct part of the road, especially when approaching and negotiating hazards?	70%	Straddling lanes. Incorrect position for right and left turns.
Progress	Do you keep up a reasonable pace and maintain good progress bearing in mind the road, traffic and weather conditions?	14%	Adequate progress not maintained when safe to do so.
Restraint	Do you show reasonable restraint and no indecision at the wheel?	20%	Insufficient restraint demonstrated.
Road signs	Do you observe road signs, approach them correctly and obey them?	36%	Failed to remember signs when asked. Failed to conform to "Stop" signs or "Keep Left" signs.
Signals	Do you give indicator and, where appropriate, hand signals at the right place and in good time?	14%	Late or misleading signals.
Speed	Do you show the ability to judge speed and distance?	26%	Excessive speed in country lanes. Failed to make adequate progress in 70 mph area.
Speed limits	Do you observe them?	22%	Exceeded speed limits.
Steering	Do you hold the steering wheel correctly? Do you pass the steering wheel through your hands?	20%	Released wheel. Crossed hands.
Traffic conditions	Do you observe traffic conditions and demonstrate anticipation?	38%	Poor anticipation. Late reaction.

Skilled driving courses

A variety of courses is available for all who wish to improve their driving in any way. The test and standards devised by the Institute of Advanced Motorists are explained on pages 104 and 105, and this spread describes what else is currently available.

Night driving course

Drivers who have recently passed the driving test can obtain a grounding in driving at night and the correct use of headlights through this short course run by the British School of Motoring.

Motorway course

In those areas with convenient access to a motorway a short course is available, run by the British School of Motoring, aimed at teaching newly-qualified drivers the rudiments of motorway driving.

Harrow Driving Centre

The Driving Centre at Harrow features a specially devised road layout situated away from public roads. This enables highly realistic experience to be acquired by those learning to drive and by those wishing to practise unfamiliar manoeuvres away from the bustle of everyday traffic. Several courses are available from this centre and include manoeuvrability for those who wish to improve their reversing and parking, caravan towing, Continental driving, car maintenance and advanced driving which includes some basic skid control techniques.

Local Authority courses

Many Local Authorities run advanced driving and car maintenance courses as evening classes. These are not expensive to attend and generally run for between eight to twelve weeks.

High performance course

This $17\frac{1}{2}$ hour course run by the British School of Motoring is the most advanced driving course currently available. It takes place on a wide variety of normal roads as well as on a race track, although even here two-way traffic rules are applied. The facility is available however, to learn cornering lines, braking and acceleration under the safest possible conditions and without being a hazard to other traffic. A session on a 'skid road' is also included in the course.

The instructor compiles a detailed report on each pupil throughout the course, and at its conclusion using the report as a guide the committee can elect the pupil to the High Performance Club.

RoSPA Advanced Drivers Association

The Royal Society for the Prevention of Accidents, in 1980, took over the administration of the former League of Safe Drivers, which was a well-established and widely-respected organisation devoted to better driving.

The original aims were retained, and these were: 'to improve the standard of driving by having a body of people who have subjected themselves to advanced driving tests conducted by examiners with the highest qualifications and who have undertaken to drive at all times according to the Highway Code, thus setting an example of courtesy and consideration'.

The principles of driving followed by the Association are those outlined in 'Roadcraft', and the standards are maintained by means of a driving test. This is administered via RoSPA's headquarters, and conducted in the driver's home area by a locally based examiner, all of whom are qualified as Police Class 1 drivers.

After the test, drivers are graded class one, two or three. Class one and two drivers have to be re-tested every three years, and class three every year. These free re-tests make this system unique, probably in the world.

As well as assessing driving skill, the test also involves questions on the Highway Code and on car mechanics. Drivers have the option of providing a spoken commentary, although this is not a rigid requirement. After the test the examiner will go through any comments with the candidate, and a full report will be sent to him from the RoSPA headquarters.

Grand touring course

The beginnings of high performance driving are taught in this British School of Motoring course. Three sessions cover driving on country roads, trunk roads and motorways.

Advanced driving course

Advanced driving courses are available through local authorities and the BSM to drivers wishing to polish and re-assess their own performance. These courses can also be tailored to the requirements of the IAM test.

ectures, models, demonstrations, and simulators are all used in driver education courses.

107

Books and films

A wealth of further information is available for those interested in driving. This is published in a variety of forms, books, magazines and films. Many will be available in local libraries, and the films can all be readily obtained. Everyone whose interest in driving has been aroused or developed by this work will find much of interest in the materials described here.

Books

Advanced Driver
Joe Kells.
Published by David and Charles.

Advanced Motoring
Institute of Advanced Motorists.
Published by Macdonald and Jane's.

Are You a Skilful Driver?
Norman Sullivan.
Published by Charles Letts.

Attention All Drivers
Jock Taylor.
Published by The Order of the Road.

Book of the Car
Published by Drive Publications.

Car Driving in Two Weeks
Lawrence Nathan, revised by Andrew M Hunt.
Published by Elliot Right Way Books.

Drivecraft
Geoffrey Godwin.
Published by Barrie and Rockliffe.

Driver Training for Young People
Ministry of Transport.
Published by HMSO.

Driving
Department of Transport.
Published by HMSO.

Driving Instructor's Handbook
T&E Wilson. Published by Elliot Right Way Books.

Driving Made Easy
Ken Jolly. Published by Macmillan and Penguin (paperback).

Driving Today. The BSM Way
Tom Wisdom and Ronald Priestly.
Published by Peter Davies.

Expert Driving The Police Way
John Miles.
Published by Peter Davies and Sphere Books (paperback).

Fitness for the Motorist
Dennis Chambers.
Published by Charles Letts.

Guide to Law for the Motorist
Peter Hughman and David Lewis.
Published by Aidfairs.

Highway Code
Published by HMSO.

Highway Code Questions and Answers
John Humphreys.
Published by Elliot Right Way Books.

How to Drive Safely
John Eldred Howard.
Penguin Books.

Know Your Traffic Signs
Published by the Department of Transport.

Lawyer in Your Car
Anthony Brigden and Stewart Patterson. Published by Temco.

Lucas make the 'L' Test Easy
Roy Johnstone.
Published by W Foulsham.

Money Saving Motoring
Published by Drive Publications.

Motoring Law A to Z
J L Thomas.
Published by Elliot Right Way Books.

Parking Law
Charles Brandreth.
Published by David and Charles.

Road Accidents. What would you do?
Dennis Chambers.
Published by Charles Letts.

Roadcraft
Published by HMSO.

Road Research—Driver Instruction
Published by the Organisation for Economic Co-operation and Development.

Road Safety Research
Published by Salford University.

An evaluation of the effectiveness of driver and traffic education in reducing road accidents among adolescents. S. Raymond and others.
An examination of the problems of continuous assessment in driver education. A M Risk.
An examination of the relevance of current educational research for driver education. A M Risk.
Notes for the course of driver education used in the Salford Road Safety Experiment. K W Jolly.
The use of accidents and traffic offences as criteria for evaluating courses in driver education. Jean Shaoul.
The use of driving tests as alternative criteria to accidents for evaluating driver education. Jean Shaoul.
The use of scholastic tests of driving knowledge and the national licensing test as criteria for evaluating the effects of driver education. Jean Shaoul.

The use of a test of driving knowledge and driving practices a criteria for evaluating the effectiveness of driver education. Jea Shaoul.

Road Test
Norman Sullivan.
Published by Fontana.

Save Money on Your Car
Stuart Bladon.
Published by Stanley Paul.

Sensible Driving
M J Hosken.
Published by David and Charle

Skilful Driver
James S Blair.
Published by Temple Press.

Sportsmanlike Driving
American Automobile Associatio
Published by McGraw Hill.

Steering Clear
E Hambert.
Published by Neville Spearma

Very Advanced Driving
A Tom Topper.
Published by Elliot Right Wa Books.

Your Driving Test and How To Pa
Published by the Department Transport.

Magazines

The following is a selected list motoring magazines whic regularly carry articles on driving

Autocar
Care on the Road
Drive
Milestones
Motor
Popular Motoring
Practical Motorist

Films

Driver's Eye View
Produced by TRRL.
Demonstrates the movements a driver's eye makes at the wheel.

Winter Driving
Produced by Shell.
Shows how motorists can ensure that their cars and driving methods can cope with winter conditions and the resultant hazards.

Night Driving
Produced by Sorel Films and sponsored by 3M.
Techniques and precautions of night driving.

Skid Sense
Produced by RHR Productions for Dunlop Rubber Company.
Skid-pan demonstrations plus sequences to explain differences in tyre construction.

This Your Life?
Produced by Avon Rubber in cooperation with RoSPA.
Michael Bentine introduces a humorous look at the care and maintenance of tyres.

The Law and Your Tyres
Produced for India Tyres.
New regulations on tyres explained.

Out of Sight—Out of Mind
Produced by the Shock Absorber Manufacturers' Association.
The dangers of driving on worn shock absorbers.

Worn Shock Absorbers are Dangerous
Produced by the European Shock Absorber Manufacturers' Association.
The effects of driving a car with worn shock absorbers in wet conditions.

Drivers—Turning right
Produced by Gulf Oil in co-operation with RoSPA. A Norman Hemsley production.
Ten per cent of accidents occur when turning right. This film demonstrates the correct drill for this manoeuvre.

Think Ahead
Produced by Gulf Oil in co-operation with RoSPA. A Norman Hemsley production.
Emphasises the need to think ahead and maintain sufficient distance between vehicles.

Nothing to Chance
Produced by Gulf Oil in co-operation with RoSPA. A Norman Hemsley production.
Demonstrates that good maintenance and good driving go hand-in-hand. Braking in articulated heavy vehicles demonstrated.

Turn to Better Driving
Produced for RoSPA in co-operation with Avon Tyres. A Norman Hemsley production.
Dick Emery (a one-time driving instructor) demonstrates with the help of models the right and wrong way of dealing with a number of driving hazards.

Road Sense
Produced by RHR Productions for the Dunlop Rubber Company.
Illustrates the right approach to everyday driving situations. Demonstrated by a police driving instructor.

Motoring Practice
Produced by Shell for the Institute of Advanced Motorists. (Sole distribution via RoSPA film library).
Every driver needs to practise. This film covers a wide range of motoring techniques.

Six Candles
Produced for the British Insurance Association.
The last two days in the life of John Smith, an insurance inspector. Although normally a good driver he meets his death through a moment's carelessness.

Ride in a car
Produced for Shell Mex and B.P. Ltd.
A family is looking for a country house by car. The film demonstrates their principles of good driving and shows children playing the 'Traffic Game'.

Motor Mania
Produced by Walt Disney Productions Ltd.
This cartoon shows that many people who behave normally as pedestrians become selfish and thoughtless behind the wheel.

Freeway Phobia (Parts I and II)
Produced by Walt Disney Productions Ltd.
Animated characters illustrate errors in motorway driving.

Defensive Driving
Produced by the Post Office.
A split second is all it takes to end a man's life.

A Testing Job
Produced by the Central Office of Information for the Ministry of Transport.
Describes the how and why of the driving test and the purpose behind the examiner's approach.

A Moment's Reflection
Produced by the Central Office of Information for the Ministry of Transport.
The importance of continuous, defensive driving and the danger of loss of concentration are shown.

Too Close For Comfort
Produced by the Central Office of Information for the Department of the Environment.
Reg Varney commentates while a Driving Instructor demonstrates how space can be preserved in normal driving conditions.

L For Logic
Produced by the Central Office of Information for the Department of the Environment.
The film illustrates that there is a reason for everything asked of a candidate who takes the driving test.

Without Due Care
Produced by the Metropolitan Police.
A twenty-four hour tour of duty by Metropolitan Police traffic officers is like a mobile chess game.

Drive Carefully, Darling
Produced by the Central Office of Information for the Department of the Environment.
A science fiction account of the consequences of ignoring the rules of safe driving. The 'action' takes place inside the driver's head.

The Motorway File
Produced by the Central Office of Information for the Department of the Environment.
A dramatised story of a fatal motorway accident and the events preceding it.

Night Call
Produced by the Central Office of Information for the Department of Transport.
The story of a motoring correspondent's search for the perfect driver. It deals with all aspects of motorway driving procedure, particularly at night or in bad weather conditions.

Index

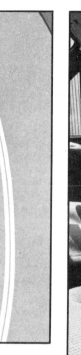

The publishers wish to thank the following individuals and organisations for their assistance in the preparation of this book:

Autocar
Britax
Britover (Continental) Limited
L Dennis
Desmo Limited
Dolland & Aitchison Limited
Ebley Tyre Services
W Edwards
Ford Motor Company Limited
Dennis Hunter Limited
Institute of Advanced Motorists
Kangol Magnet Limited
Kemble Skid Training School
K L Automotive Products Limited
The Metropolitan Police
Royal Society for the Prevention of Accidents
Transport and Road Research Laboratory